비서를 위한

비즈니스 영어

Business English for Secretaries

서문

　이 책은 학생들이 앞으로 사회에 진출해서 비서 업무를 할 때 필요한 비즈니스 영어를 구어와 문어 양 측면에서 다루고 있다. 비서가 되기를 희망하는 학생들의 요구에 부응해 전화 통화, 예약, 손님 접대 외에 비즈니스 레터, 이메일, 일정표 작성을 주된 내용으로 구성하였다. 개정판을 내며, 급변하는 온라인, 모바일 사무환경에 맞추어 업무를 처리할 수 있도록 관련 내용을 강화하였다. 전문 행정 비서 업무를 염두에 두고, 프리젠테이션과 토론시에 사용되는 표현까지 다루고 있어 일반적인 비즈니스 영어책이라 해도 큰 무리가 없을 것으로 생각된다.

　학생들이 외국어를 더 잘 습득하기 위해서는 외국어 학습이 현실의 경험들과 연관이 있어야 한다. 실제 상황을 그대로 반영하는 대화문을 공부하면서 현재의 학습 내용이 현실적으로 느껴질 때 흥미를 가지고 보다 많은 내용을 기억할 수 있게 된다. 이 책에서는 학생들이 사회에 나아가 직면할 수 있는 여러 가지 현실적 상황이 그대로 영어 대화문으로 정리되어 있다. 또한 학생들이 취업을 준비하는 데 도움을 주고자 이력서와 커버레터 쓰는 방법도 간단히 설명하였으며, 면접 준비에 도움을 주기 위해 예상 질문과 답변의 예문들을 수록하였다. 의사소통 수단으로 이메일의 중요성이 커지는 현실을 반영하여 이메일의 구성과 표현을 깊이 있게 다룬 것은 기존의 비서영어 교재와의 차이점이다. 현실 상황에 맞게 구성된 대화문이나 각종 샘플 서식들을 공부하면서 학생들이 사회에 나아가 실용적인 영어를 적절히 구사하게 되기를 희망한다.

　끝으로 책을 쓰는 동안 옆에서 지켜 보며 인내해 주고 격려해 준 가족들과 책을 펴내도록 도와 주신 한올 출판사분들께 감사의 마음을 전한다.

CONTENTS

UNIT 1

Making Calls / Receiving Calls

UNIT 2

Hosting

coNteNtS

UNIT 3 — Making Reservations

CONTENTS

UNIT 4 — Office Works & Computer / Machine Problems

UNIT 5 — Business Letter / E-mail

CONTENTS

UNIT 6

Presentation

coNteNts

BUSINESS ENGLIISH for SECRETARIES

Making Calls
/
Receiving Calls

Unit
1

Making Calls / Receiving Calls

업무의 많은 부분이 전화 통화로 이루어지므로 기본적으로 전화를 걸고 받고 연결하는 것 뿐 아니라 전화로 약속을 잡고, 메시지 받고 남길 수 있어야 한다. 또한 전화상 대화에서 적절한 표현이나 예의에 맞는 어법으로 영어를 구사할 수 있도록 준비하여야 한다.

1 전화 연결

A   Good morning, Mr. Robert Smith's office. May I help you?

B   I'd like to speak to Mr. Smith.

A   Can I ask who's calling please?

B   This is Grace Lee from Econet Company.

A   Just a moment, please. I'll transfer your call.

B   Thank you.

- speak to ~   전화로 ~와 이야기하다.

- this is~   전화로 자신을 호칭할 때는 I'm 보다는 This is 를 쓴다.

- Just a moment = Hold on a moment   (끊지 말고) 기다려주세요.

  Hang up   "전화를 끊다"와 구별해야 한다.

- transfer the call   전화를 연결하다.

  put A through   A를 (전화) 연결하다.

- Who is calling, please?   전화 건 상대방이 누구인지 묻는 표현. 보다 더 정중하게 물을 때는 Can I ask나 May I ask를 앞에 붙여서 May I ask who's calling please? 라고 한다.

A	Hello, you've reached the Accounting Dept. How can I help you?
B	Can I speak to Michelle Reagan, please?
A	Certainly. Who's calling please?
B	My name is Mike Wilson.
A	Just a second. I'll see if she's available. (To Ms. Reagan) Hello, Ms. Reagan? I've got Mike Wilson on the phone for you. … I'll put him through. (To Mr. Wilson) Mr. Wilson? Thank you for waiting. Ms. Reagan will be right with you.

- ⏻ **reach** (전화로) 연락이 닿다. 회화에서 흔히 쓰는 표현이므로 꼭 익혀 둔다.

- ⏻ **Accounting Dept.** 회계부

- ⏻ **How can I help you?** 무엇을 도와 드릴까요?

  = May I help you? 또는 Is there anything I can do for you?

- ⏻ **Just a second** hold on a minute, wait a second 과 같은 표현이다.

- ⏻ **I'll see if she's available** 그가 (전화 받는 것이) 가능한지 알아보겠습니다.

- ⏻ **I've got A on the phone for you** 당신께 A로부터 전화가 와 있습니다.

  You're wanted on the phone from A라고 하기도 한다.

- ⏻ **A will be right with you.** A씨가 곧 전화 받으실 것입니다.

A　　Secretarial Department. Jisoo Kim speaking. May I help you?

B　　Good morning. May I speak to Mr. Parker?

A　　Who is calling, please?

B　　This is John Scott of Tops Textile.

A　　Hold the line please.

　　　(To Mr. Parker) Mr. Parker, there is a call from Mr. Scott of Tops Textile on line 1.

C　　Put him through.

A　　Yes, Mr. Parker.

　　　(To Mr. Scott) Mr. Parker is on the line. Please go ahead.

- Secretarial Department　비서실
- Hold the line　전화를 끊지 말고 듣고 계세요.

  Hold on, Stay on the line 등으로도 표현하며, 조금 오래 기다리게 하는 경우에는 May I put you on hold?라고 하는 것이 좋다.

- There is a call from ~　~에게서 전화 와 있습니다.
- put A through (to B)　A를 (B에게) 연결하다.
- go ahead　(전화에서) 말씀하세요

  (상대방을 재촉하여 권하는 경우) 자, 어서 하세요, 계속하세요.

7

A   Could I have the Public Relations Department?

B   Certainly, sir, but do you have a specific person you want to speak to in Public Relations?

A   Yes, Mr. John Smith, please.

B   Hold on please...... I'm sorry but his line is busy at the moment. His extension number is 5724. You can speak to him directly if you call this number.

A   Thank you.

⏻ Public Relations Department   홍보부

⏻ His line is busy   그는 통화 중이십니다.
   = The line is busy.

⏻ extension number   내선번호 (Ext.)

참고

전화 관련 용어

- **cellular phone** 핸드폰
  cell phone 또는 mobile phone 이라고도 한다.
- **direct line** 직통 전화선
- **international call / overseas call** 국제 전화
- **international roaming / overseas roaming** 국제 로밍
- **data roaming** 데이터 로밍
- **long-distance call** 장거리 전화
- **local call** 시내 전화
- **country code** 국가 번호
- **area code** 지역 번호
- **collect call** 수신자 부담 전화
- **toll-free call** 무료 전화 800 등으로 시작
- **conference call** 컨퍼런스 콜. 세 명 이상이 동시에 연결되어 회의할 수 있는 전화로 화상 전화 시스템이 연결되어 있는 경우도 있다.

A	Hello. This is Janet Morris from Apple Holdings. May I speak to Mr. Jeff Parker?
B	May I ask what you're calling for?
A	I am returning Mr. Parker's call.
B	Can you hold for a second?
A	Yes, thank you.
B	(To Mr. Jeff Parker) Mr. Parker, Janet Morris is calling you. (To caller) Mr. Parker will be right with you. ……
C	Hello. I've been expecting your call.

- **Holdings**   지주 회사
- **May I ask what you're calling for?**   용건을 묻는 표현
  What is it about, please? What is this call about? May I ask what this is about?
- **return one's call**   (~의 전화에 대해) 회답 전화를 하다.
- **A is calling you**   A가 전화하셨습니다. (A씨 전화입니다.)
  You are wanted on the phone (from A) : (A에게서) 전화 왔습니다.
- **Mr. Parker will be right with you**   Parker씨가 곧 전화 받으실 겁니다.
- **I've been expecting your call.**   전화 기다리고 있었습니다.

A Secretarial Department. Lesley Jang speaking.

B This is Cyndy Jung. Please put me through to Mr. Smith.

A I'm sorry, but he's with a client and asked not to be disturbed unless it's urgent.

B I hate to ask you, but could you please interrupt him for me?
I have an urgent matter to discuss with him.

A Well, let me check, but I doubt I'll be able to put you through.
(To Mr. Smith) Cyndy Jung is on the line. She said she had an urgent matter to discuss with you.

C All right. Put her through.

ὃ put A through (to B)　A를 (B에게) 연결하다

ὃ asked not to be disturbed unless it's urgent.　급하지 않으면 연결하지 말라고 하셨습니다.

ὃ I hate to ask you but ~　이런 부탁 드리기는 싫지만.

ὃ I doubt I'll be able to put you through　연결해 드릴 수 있을지 모르겠습니다.

ὃ ~ is on the line　누구 전화가 와있습니다.

ὃ interrupt　방해하다.

ὃ Could you please interrupt him for me?　방해가 되더라도 전화를 받으라고 해 주시겠습니까?

A   Hello, this is Perez calling from St. Peter's Hospital. Can I speak to Dr. Seuss?

B   I'm afraid he's not available now. He's in a meeting at the moment.

A   What time do you expect him back?

B   He won't be free till 6 p.m.

A   Then, could you ask him to call me back? My number is 387-8902.

B   Sure, Ms. Perez. I'll repeat your number, 387- 8902.
      I'll ask him to call you back as soon as he's free.

A   Thank you for your help.

⏻ **What time do you expect him back?**   그가 언제 돌아올 것 같습니까?

⏻ **won't (will not) be free till ~**   ~ 까지는 시간이 없을 것이다.

⏻ **call someone back**   ~ 에게 다시 전화 걸어 주다.

⏻ **I'll repeat your number**   전화번호를 듣고 메모한 후에는 확인을 위해 꼭 자신이 쓴 대로 읽어서 들려 주어야 한다.

⏻ **as soon as~**   ~ 하자마자

A	Good afternoon. Mr. Hawker's office.
B	This is Jisoo Kim from First Securities. May I speak to Mr. Hawker?
A	I'm sorry, but he's gone for the day.
B	Is there any way I can contact him now? I have some urgent matters to discuss with him.
A	I'll have him return your call as soon as I locate him, if that's all right.
B	Yes, please. I'll be waiting for his call. Thanks. I appreciate it.
A	You're welcome.

◔ ecurities   증권회사

◔ He's gone for the day   퇴근하다. =He's left for the day.

◔ locate   찾아내다

◔ if that's all right   괜찮으시다면

◔ Thanks. I appreciate it.   정말 감사합니다. (동의어를 반복함으로써 의미 강조할 수 있다.)

A   Hello. This is Steve Rice from Apple Electronics.

        May I speak to Mr. Kim please?

B   I'm sorry, but Mr. Kim went on a business trip to Dubai.

        He left everything up to Mr. Scott, so he can help you.

        May I put you through to him?

A   Well, I'd rather speak to Mr. Kim directly. How can I reach him?

B   Then you can contact him directly at 010-555-3567.

- ⏻ go on a business trip (to 장소) (어디로) 출장가다.
- ⏻ leave A up to B A를 B에 맡기다.
- ⏻ I'd rather I would rather 차라리 ~ 하겠다. 더 낫다.
- ⏻ reach (전화 등으로) 연락하다.
- ⏻ contact 연락을 취하다.

상사가 부재중인 경우 안내

- **He is not in at the moment.**   지금 안 계십니다.
- **He's not at his desk.**   지금 자리에 안 계십니다.
- **He's not in today.**   오늘은 외근입니다.
- **I'm sorry, but he's out now.**   죄송하지만, 지금 외부에 계십니다.
- **He's off today. Today is his day off.**   오늘은 쉬는 날입니다.
- **He's (away) on a business trip.**   출장 중입니다.
- **He's out of town on business.**   출장 가셨습니다.
- **He's just stepped out.**   방금 나가셨습니다.
- **He's gone (또는 left) for the day.**   퇴근하셨습니다.
- **He's out to (또는 for) lunch.**   점심 식사하러 가셨습니다.
- **He's just stepped out for lunch.**   식사하러 막 나가셨습니다.
- **He is busy (또는 tied up) now.**   지금 바쁘십니다.
- **He's in a meeting.**   미팅 중이십니다.
- **He's in an interview.**   인터뷰 중이십니다.
- **He is with a client. He is talking to a client.**   손님과 말씀 중이십니다.
- **He is on the phone.**   통화 중이십니다.
- **He's on another line at the moment.**   지금 다른 전화 받고 계십니다.

상사가 통화중인 경우

A   Good morning. Mr. Smith's office. May I help you?

B   This is Eugene Kim of Morris Securities. May I speak to Mr. Smith?

A   I'm afraid he's on another line.

B   How long will he be on the phone?

A   It will take a few minutes. May I put you on hold?

B   Well, could you have him call me when he's done?

A   Certainly.

ᵁ **be on another line**　다른 전화를 받다. 통화 중이다.

ᵁ **How long will he be on the phone?**　통화가 얼마나 길어질까요?
Do you think it is going to be long?　통화가 길어질 것 같은가요?

ᵁ **May I have put you on hold?** : hold on의 의미. 상대방을 좀 오래 기다리게 할 경우에는 "just a minute" 이나 "hold on" 보다는 "May I put you on hold?" 또는 "May I put your call on hold?", "Let me put you on hold" 라고 하여 대기시키는 것이 좋다.

ᵁ **have A call B**　A로 하여금 B에게 전화하게 하다.
make A call B, ask A to call B로도 할 수 있다.

ᵁ **certainly**　알았습니다. 물론이죠.

A　I'm sorry, but he is on the phone right now. Would you hold for a moment?

……

I'm afraid it will take a little more time.

B　Please ask him to call me as soon as he gets off the line.

A　Could I have your contact information?

B　He has my phone number.

I'm afraid it will take a little more time.　통화가 좀 길어질 것 같습니다

as soon as he gets off the line.　통화 끝나는 대로

contact information　연락처

A   TNN Company, Jina Kim speaking.

B   This is Alex White from Intel Company. Can I speak to Mr. Sean Park?

A   Mr. White, I'm afraid Mr. Park is in a meeting at the moment. Would you like to leave a message?

B   Yes, please tell him to call me back.

A   Certainly I will. Does he know your number?

B   Yes, he does.

A   May I have it, just in case?

B   It's 354-445-8824.

A   Let me repeat it. 354-445-8824.

B   It's correct.

A   Thank you. I'll tell him to call you back as soon as he can.

○ at the moment   지금은 (now)

○ May I have it (또는 your number), just in case?   만약의 경우에 대비해서 제게 전화번호를 좀 알려 주시겠어요?

○ just in case   혹시, 만약의 경우에 대비해서

○ take a message   전화 메시지를 받다.

leave a message   전화 메시지를 남기다.

Would you like to leave a message?   메시지 남기기시겠습니까?

May I take your message?   메시지를 받아드릴까요?

A   General Affairs Department. Heyjin Kim speaking.

B   This is Lisa Choi. I'm with the Star Company. Is Mr. Smith available?

A   I'm sorry, Mr. Smith is in a meeting at the moment.

B   Do you know what time he'll be free?

A   He should be free this afternoon.

B   May I leave a message?

A   Certainly. May I have your name?

B   It's Lisa Choi.

A   How do you spell your name?

B   L-I-S-A C-H-O-I.

○ General Affairs Department   총무부

○ I'm with ~ company.   저는 ~ 회사에서 일합니다.

○ should   ~ 틀림없이 ~ 할 것이다.

○ free   시간이 나는, 한가한

○ How do you spell your name?   당신 이름의 철자는 어떻게 쓰나요?

A   Good morning. Apple Software, Marketing Division.

B   Hello, This is Jordan Jason from Green Computers.
Is Ms. Taylor in?

A   Just a second please. … I'm sorry, she's not at her desk at the moment. Can I take a message?

B   Yes, could you ask her to call me?

A   I'd be happy to. You said your name was Mr. Jason?

B   That's right. Jordan Jason.

A   And, you're with Green Computers?

B   Right.

A   Does Ms. Taylor know your number?

B   I think so, but let me give it to you, just in case. It's 254-0552.

A   Fine. Let me read that back to you. It's 254-0552.

B   That's right.

A   I'll have her return your call.

B   Thanks.

💡 **Is ~ in?**   May I speak to ~? 와 같은 상황에서 사용할 수 있으며, "~씨 계신가요?"의 의미이다. "Is ~ available?" (~씨 전화통화 가능합니까?) 로도 말할 수 있다.

💡 **I'd be happy to**   기꺼이요.

💡 **just in case**   만일의 경우를 생각하여, 혹시 모르니

💡 **return one's call**   (~의 전화에 대해)회답 전화를 하다

💡 **Let me read that back to you.**   (받아 적은 다음) 읽어 보겠습니다.
Let me repeat it 이라고도 한다.
상대가 적은 것을 확인하고 싶을 때는 Could you read that back to me? 라고 한다.

💡 **I'll have her return your call.**   제가 그녀보고 당신께 전화 걸라고 하겠습니다.
= I'll have her call you back.

참고

전화메시지 남겨보기

부재 중에 걸려 온 전화 메시지를 받기 위해 자신의 전화에 자동 응답기(answering machine) 메시지를 녹음할 필요가 있으며, 또한 자동 응답기에 자신의 용건을 남겨야 할 때가 있다. 특히 우리 나라에서 미국이나 유럽 지역에 전화 해야 할 경우는 시차 때문에 자동 응답기를 이용해야 하는 경우가 많을 수 있으므로 여기에 대해 준비해 본다.

● 전화 메시지 1 ●

Answering Machine   You've reached 010 435 8734. I can't come to the phone right now, so please leave a message after the beep. I will get back to you as soon as possible. Thanks. Beep!

Message   Hi, this is Grace Lee. I'm calling to confirm the meeting with you. Please call me back any time soon. Just in case, my phone number is 010 485 7400. Bye.

● 전화 메시지 2 ●

Answering Machine   Thank you for calling St. Mary Hospital. All of our operators are busy at the moment. Please wait for the next available operator.

● 전화 메시지 3 ●

Answering Machine   You've reached Moda Company. The office is now closed. Our hours are from 8:15 to 4:45, Monday to Wednesday and Friday. On Thursdays, we're open from 10:45 to 4:45. To repeat this message, please press star and four. Thank you.

- **reach**   (전화)로 연락이 닿다.
- **get back to someone**   ～에게 연락하다. (회화에서 많이 쓰인다.)
- **beep**   전화의 삐 소리
- **operator**   전화 교환원

참고

전화 걸어 달라고 요청할 때

- **Can you give me a call back?**
  저에게 전화 걸어줄 수 있습니까?

- **Can you call me when you are free?**
  시간 나면 전화해 줄 수 있으신가요?

- **Feel free to call me back any time.**
  언제라도 저에게 전화해 주세요.

- **Can you ask her to call me back?**
  그녀보고 저에게 전화하라고 해 주세요.

전화 메모 남기기

상사가 부재 중에 전화를 받았을 때는 누가, 언제, 왜 전화를 했는지 메모해 두어야 한다. 또한 전화 건 사람의 신분과 연락 가능한 전화 번호도 꼭 기입해 둔다.

To   :   Mr. Anderson Cooper

Date :   Feb. 25th

Time :   3:15 p.m.

WHILE YOU WERE OUT

Mr. / Ms. :   Ms. Magan Forbes

Company :   BNG Consulting Corporation

Phone   :   1-612-871-1020

☐ Telephoned

☐ Will call again

☑ Please call back

☐ Returned your call

☐ Called to see you

☐ Urgent

Message : to discuss the status of the AP2 project.

Taken by : Jina Kim

A   This is Ryan Kim. Can I talk to Sean O'Brien?

B   Sorry? Can you speak up a little? You sound miles away.

A   It's a bad line. I'll hang up and call you back.
      …… Hello, this is Ryan Kim again.

⏻ **Sorry?**   I beg your pardon? 또는 Pardon? Pardon me? 는 상대방의 말을 잘 못 알아 들었을 때 뭐라구요? 하는 표현이다.

⏻ **speak up**   큰 소리로 말하다.

⏻ **You sound miles away.**   소리가 멀리 들립니다.

⏻ **bad line, bad connection**   연결이 안 좋다.

⏻ **hang up**   전화를 끊다.

⏻ **This is …again.**   (전화 끊은 후 다시 전화 걸었을 때) ~ 입니다.

A   Is this Hanshin Corporation?

B   Yes, it is.

A   This is Nick Denton of Eric Industries. Can I speak to Ms. Ellis?

B   It's very noisy here. Could you speak up a bit?

A   I'm afraid we have a crossed line. I'll hang up and call again.

B   All right.

Business English for Secretaries

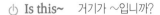

⟳ **Is this~**   거기가 ~입니까?

⟳ **We have a crossed line**   혼선이 되었습니다.
     같은 상황에서 "The lines seem to be mixed up." 이라고 할 수도 있다.

25

A   Can I speak to Matthew White?

B   Matthew White? I'm afraid you must have the wrong number. There's no one here by that name.

A   I'm sorry.

⏻ have the wrong number   전화를 잘못 걸다.

⏻ must v.   —임에 틀림없다.

⏻ No one here by that name   그런 이름 가진 사람은 없습니다.

8 전화로 약속하기

> A   Good morning, Laura Yoon speaking.
>
> B   Good morning, Ms. Yoon. This is Paul Howard from Klein Company. I'd like to see you to discuss the Panda project. When would be convenient for you?
>
> A   How about this Friday three o'clock in my office?
>
> B   I'm afraid I have a previous appointment then. Can we make it at 4:30?
>
> A   Yes, that's fine with me.
>
> B   Good. Then I'll visit your office tomorrow at 4:30.
>
> A   I'll see you then, Mr. Howard.

- **When would be convenient for you?** 언제가 편한가요?

  = When would suit you?

  = What time would be convenient for you?

  * **Where would be convenient for you?** : 어디가 편하신가요?

- **convenient**   (시간이) 편한

  사람을 주어로 쓰지 않는 것에 유의한다.

- **previous appointment**   선약

- **make it at ~**   ~(시간)에 약속을 잡다.

- **expect someone**   ―를 기다리다. 기대하다.

- **free**   시간이 있다. 한가하다.

- **That's fine with me.**   좋습니다.

Business English for Secretaries

A　Mr. Stone's Office.

B　Hello, can I speak to Matthew Stone, please?

A　I'm afraid he's in a meeting now.

B　My name is Hugo Shin. I'd like to arrange an appointment to see him.

A　Could you hold on for a second, please?

　　I'll just check my appointment book. … When is convenient for you?

B　Sometime next week. What about next Thursday?

A　He's free in the afternoon around 4 o'clock.

B　That's fine with me. Then let's make it at four.

A　Mr. Shin, Mr. Stone will expect you next Thursday at 4 o'clock.

B　Thank you.

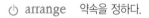

↻ arrange　약속을 정하다.

↻ What about ~　~ 이 어떠세요? 시간, 장소 등을 제안할 때 쓰이는 요긴한 표현이다. (=How about~?)

↻ appointment book (schedule book)　스케줄을 관리하는 수첩

↻ around　~시경, 쯤

A   Good afternoon. Ms. Morgan's office.

B   This is Mr. Jason's secretary calling.
I'm afraid that Mr. Jason will not be able to see Ms. Morgan at two o'clock today.
We're terribly sorry but something urgent has come up.

A   Oh, I see.

B   Thank you for your understanding. And Mr. Jason wants to reschedule his appointment. We'll accommodate Ms. Morgan's schedule.

A   Let me check her schedule first and then I'll call you back.

B   Okay, I'll be expecting your call.

What time would be the most convenient?   몇 시가 가장 편한가요?

I can accommodate your schedule.   당신 일정에 맞출 수 있어요.

  = I can arrange my schedule to fit yours.

29

A   Hello. This is Mr. Jackson's secretary. May I talk to Mr. Martin's secretary?

B   This is she speaking.

A   Mr. Jackson would like to see Mr. Martin sometime next week.

B   Well, let's see... either Monday or Thursday would be fine.

A   Monday would be preferable. Would that be O.K. with Mr. Martin?

B   Yes, that's good.

A   What time would be the most convenient for Mr. Martin?

B   How about 2:00?

A   Yes, that would be fine.

⏻ This is she speaking. 접니다.

⏻ either A or B A나 B 둘 중 아무것이나

⏻ preferable 보다 나은

A   This is Sandra Hyun of ABC Electronics calling. I'm calling on behalf of Mr. Cullen.

B   I see. What can I do for you, Ms. Hyun?

A   Mr. Cullen would like to see Mr. James this Friday at 10:00 at your office.
     Would that be satisfactory?

B   I think he can make it. I'll confirm it with Mr. James and call you back.

A   When can you let me know by?

B   I'll let you know by 4 o'clock for sure.

Business English for Secretaries

⟳ on behalf of ~   ~ 를 대신해서, 대표해서

⟳ satisfactory   만족할 만한

⟳ confirm   (약속을) 확인하다.

⟳ When can you let me know by?   언제까지 저에게 알려 줄 수 있습니까?

⟳ for sure   확실히

31

A   Hello. This is Helen O'Grady from Nice Industries calling. Can I speak to Mr. Brown's secretary?

B   Speaking. How may I help you?

A   I'm calling to let you know that the meeting scheduled for tomorrow 10 a.m. will be postponed due to a scheduling conflict.

B   Then, until when will it be postponed?

A   It is not yet decided. I'll let you know as soon as possible.

B   Thank you. I'll make sure Mr. Brown gets the message.

- Speaking 접니다
- I'm calling to ~ ~하려고 전화합니다.
- postpone 연기하다.
- due to 때문에
- scheduling conflict 스케줄 상의 마찰, 스케줄 상의 문제
- Then until when will it be postponed? 그럼 언제까지 연기되나요?
- I'll make sure he gets the message. 그에게 꼭 메시지를 전달하겠습니다.

A　Hello. May I speak to Mr. Chang?

B　Yes. This is he speaking.

A　This is Jane Smith. I am calling regarding your message.

B　Yes, Jane. I called you to see if we could reschedule our appointment.

A　Then when would be convenient for you?

B　Is it okay to meet on Friday at one?

A　Let's see. It's fine with me.

B　Sorry for the inconvenience.

A　Don't worry about it. Then I'll see you on Friday.

● Business English for Secretaries

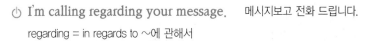

I'm calling regarding your message.　메시지보고 전화 드립니다.
regarding = in regards to 〜에 관해서

reschedule　약속을 다시 잡다.

inconvenience　불편함

9 핸드폰으로 통화하기

Cellular phone

A	Ms. Lee. Could you tell me..... (The sound goes on and off)
B	I'm sorry. I'm in the underground parking lot and there's bad reception. Your voice goes on and off.
A	I see. Could you call...... (The sound goes on and off)
B	Now I am in an elevator. I am losing you. Let me call you back.
A	Okay, but I am going out now. Please call me on my mobile.

- The sound goes on and off 소리가 들렸다 안 들렸다 한다.
- underground parking lot 지하주차장
  (지하 2층 주차장은 second basement parking lot 또는 second basement level parking lot)
- reception (라디오, TV, 전화의) 수신 상태
  There's bad reception 수신상태가 안 좋다.
- I'm losing you 통화중 소리가 멀어지거나 잘 안 들리게 될 때 이렇게 말한다.
- call me on my mobile = call me on my mobile phone 휴대폰으로 전화하다.

A   Can I talk to you for a minute?

B   Well fine, but what is it about?

A   I have something to report.

B   Please make it quick.

A   It's about our project. Several problems have come up. They are legally complicated.

B   My battery is almost dead.
     I am on my way back to the office. Let's talk about them in person.

○ make it quick (brief)   (용건만) 간단히 말하다.

○ My battery is almost dead.   배터리다 거의 다 닳았다.

○ I am on my way back to the office   사무실로 돌아가는 길이다.

○ talk about them in person   직접 만나서 그것에 대해 이야기 하다.

A   I can't find an outlet. I have to recharge my cell phone.

B   Here is a wall outlet. Plug it in.

ⓘ outlet = electrical outlet = power outlet   콘센트

ⓘ wall outlet = wall electrical outlet   벽에 있는 콘센트

ⓘ plug something in   ~의 플러그를 꽂다

ⓘ Plug something into something   ~을 ~에 연결하다

핸드폰 배터리

- **I have 10 percent battery left.** 배터리가 10% 남았다.
- **My battery is nearly out.** 배터리가 거의 없다.
- **My battery is getting low.** 배터리가 없어지고 있다.
- **My battery is low.** 배터리가 얼마 없다.
- **My phone ran out of battery.** 전화기 배터리가 나갔다.
- **My battery is dead. My battery is flat. My battery has run out.**
  배터리가 나갔다.
- **My battery is charged.** 배터리가 충전되었다.
- **My battery is fully charged.** 배터리가 가득 충전되었다.
- **My battery is half charged.** 배터리가 절반 충전되었다.
- **I'll call you back after charging my battery.**
  배터리 충전하고 전화하겠습니다.

Business English for Secretaries

Months of the Year

January	Jan.	July	July
February	Feb.	August	Aug.
March	Mar.	September	Sept.
April	Apr.	October	Oct.
May	May	November	Nov.
June	June	December	Dec.

Days of the Week

Sunday	SU
Monday	M
Tuesday	T
Wednesday	W
Thursday	TH
Friday	F
Saturday	SA

BUSINESS
ENGLiISH for
SECRETARIES

Hosting

Hosting

손님이 직접 사무실로 찾아온 경우 손님을 정중하게 접대한다. 약속이 되어 있는 손님을 안내하고, 약속을 하지 않고 온 손님에 대해서 적절하게 대처할 수 있어야 할 것이다. 이 장에서는 손님을 기다리게 하는 표현, 차를 접대하거나, 위치를 안내 하는 표현 등을 연습한다.

1 손님 접대

A   How may I help you?

B   I'm Grace Lee from Econet Company. I'd like to see Ms. Chang in the Marketing Department.

A   Do you have an appointment?

B   Yes, I do.

A   Could you please have a seat and wait a little bit? She'll be with you in five minutes. Would you like something to drink?

B   Coffee, please.

A   How would you like it?

B   With sugar, please. Thank you.

A   You're welcome.

Business English for Secretaries

ⓘ **Do you have an appointment?** 약속이 되어 있으십니까?

ⓘ **have a seat** 자리에 앉다. = take a seat

ⓘ **Would you like something to drink?** 마실 것 좀 드시겠습니까?
회사에서 뿐 아니라 가정, 식당 등 어느 곳에서도 자주 쓰이는 표현이다.

ⓘ **How would you like it?** (커피를) 어떻게 해 드릴까요?
(=How would you like your coffee?)

with sugar 설탕만 넣기

with cream and sugar 크림과 설탕 넣기

just black 블랙으로

strong   진하게

mild / weak   연하게

herb tea   허브차

green tea   녹차

tea   홍차

ginseng tea   인삼차

A   Good morning. May I help you?

B   Yes, I'd like to see Mr. Miller.

A   Is Mr. Miller expecting you?

B   Yes. I have an appointment. I'm Robert Johnson of Ace Computer.

A   Would you please have a seat over there for a moment?

B   Thank you.

A   (To Mr. Miller) Mr. Robert Johnson of Ace Computer would like to see you.

C   Please send him in.

A   Yes.

(To Mr. Johnson) Thank you for waiting, Mr. Johnson. Mr. Miller is expecting you.

Please come with me.

- Is A expecting B?   A가 B가 오는 것을 알고 있나요?

- would you please~   ~ 하시겠습니까?

- over there   저쪽으로

- send him in   안으로 들여보내세요.

- Please come with me.   이쪽으로 오세요.

    = Would you come this way please?

43

A Good afternoon. May I help you, sir?

B Yes, I have an appointment with Ms. Woods at three.

A Are you Mr. Radford of Comtech Industries?

B Yes, that's right.

A You are right on time. Would you please have a seat? I'll tell Ms. Woods that you are here.

(through interphone) Ms. Woods, Mr. Radford of Comtech Industries is here for his three o'clock appointment.

C Please show him in.

A Yes.

(To Mr. Radford) Ms. Woods is expecting you. Please go right in.

- have an appointment (with A) (A와) 약속되어 있다.
- You are right on time. 정각에 오셨군요.
- A is here A가 여기에 와 계십니다.
- show A in A를 안으로 안내하세요.
- go right in 들어가세요.

3   약속되어 있지 않은 손님 응대

A   Good morning. May I help you?

B   I am Kelly Brook of Boston Securities. I'd like to see Mr. Cadena.

A   Do you have an appointment with him?

B   I'm afraid not.

A   Actually he is tied up at the moment. But I'll see if he is available.

B   Thank you.

A   Not at all.
(To Mr. Cadena) Ms. Kelly Brook of Boston Securities is here to see you.

C   I'm sorry, but I have to attend the board meeting right now.
Would you have her call me anytime after two o'clock this afternoon?

A   I certainly will.
(To Ms. Brook) I'm sorry, but he is scheduled to attend the board meeting. Please call him after two o'clock.

B   Thank you.

A   You're welcome.

- Do you have an appointment with A   A와 약속하셨습니까?
- be tied up   매우 바쁘다.

- board meeting   이사회 회의
- have A call B   A로 하여금 B에게 전화하게 하다.
  (have는 ~하게 시키다 의 사역동사)
- be scheduled to   ~하기로 예정되다.

4 방문 손님의 용건 확인

A   Good morning. May I help you?

B   Good morning. Is Mr. Brown in?

A   May I ask your name and the nature of your business?

B   I am John Kim of CNG Life Insurance. I'd like to see him for a few minutes.

A   I'm sorry Mr. Kim, but could you let me know the nature of your business, too?

B   I'd like to talk to him about our new insurance product.

A   I see. I'll see if he's available. One moment, please……
     I'm sorry but he is not available.
     Please make an appointment before you visit him.

B   I will. Here's my business card. Could you hand it to him?

A   Sure.

○ May I ask the nature of your business?   무슨 용건으로 오셨습니까?

○ insurance product   보험 상품

○ make an appointment   약속하다

○ business card   명함

○ hand A to B   A를 B에게 주다.

 참고

명함 / 연락처 받기

- Can I have your business card?
  Sure/ No problem.

- Can I get your phone number or e-mail address?
  My phone number and e-mail address are on my business card.

- You can reach me by calling the number on my business card.

5   일찍 온 손님 응대

A   Good morning. May I help you?

B   Good morning. I have an appointment with Ms. Campbell at 10 o'clock.

A   Oh, yes. Are you Mr. Lee from Comtech Korea?

B   Yes, I am.

A   We've been expecting you. But you are a little early for your appointment.
Ms. Campbell is with a client. So you'll have to wait for about 20 minutes. Would you please have a seat over here?

B   Thank you.

A   Would you care for some coffee?

B   Yes, please. Thanks.

⏻ have an appointment (with A)   (A와) 약속이 되어있다.

⏻ care for ~   ~을 좋아하다.

Would you care for some coffee? : 커피 드시겠어요?

= Would you like some coffee?

6 방문객을 직접 안내

A　Good morning. May I help you?

B　Good morning. I have an appointment with Ms. Brown.

A　Are you Mr. Kim from Ace Motors?

B　Yes, I am.

A　Ms. Brown is expecting you. Let me show you over. This way, please.

- ☼ show (a person) over　남에게 장소를 안내하다.
- ☼ This way, please.　이쪽으로 오세요.
  = Would you come this way, please?

A   Are you Mr. Wilson of Star Electronics?

B   Yes, I am.

A   Mr. Brown is expecting you. I'll take you up to his office.

B   Thank you.

A   You're welcome. Would you get on the elevator, please?

……

Would you step out, please?

……

(knock on the door)

Mr. Wilson of Star Electronics is here.

C   Come in.

A   Please go right in, Mr. Wilson.

⏻ take ~ : ～를 데리고 가다.

 bring ~ : ～를 데리고 오다.

⏻ get on : 타다

⏻ Would you get on the elevator, please?
 (승강기에 타며) 엘리베이터에 타시겠습니까?

⏻ Would you step out, please? Would you get off, please?
 (승강기에서 내리면서) 내리시겠습니까?

> A   I'm looking for Ms. Johnson's office. I was told that it is on this floor.
>
> B   I'm sorry, but her office moved to the fifth floor.
> Take the elevator over there.
>
> A   Thank you.
>
> B   You're welcome.

⟳ **I was told that ~**   ~라고 들었습니다.

⟳ **move to**   ~ 로 이사하다. 이동하다.

⟳ **take the elevator**   엘리베이터를 타다.
에스컬레이터, 계단을 이용하는 경우도 각각 take the escalator, take the stairs 로 표현한다.

Unit 2 Hosting

A   Could you tell me where the restroom is?

B   Turn right at the end of the hall. It's next to the vending machine.
    You can't miss it.

A   Thank you.

⚬ **Could you tell me where A is?**   A가 어디 있는지 말씀해 주시겠어요?

   where <u>A is</u> 의 순서에 유의한다.

⚬ **restroom**   화장실. toilet 이라고 하지 않는다.

⚬ **turn right**   오른쪽으로 돌다.

⚬ **the end of the hall**   복도 끝

⚬ **It's next to ~**   옆에 있습니다

   opposite   반대편에

   before   전에

   behind   뒤에

⚬ **vending machine**   자동 판매기

⚬ **You can't miss it.** : 쉽게 찾을 수 있을 것입니다.

53

A   Excuse me, how can I get to the Sales Department?

B   Go straight along this corridor, and then turn left at the first corner.

     You will find it on your right.

A   Thank you.

B   My pleasure.

○ How can I get to   ～ 로 어떻게 갑니까?

○ Go straight along ~   ～을 따라 쭉 가세요

○ corridor   복도 =hallway

○ turn left (right) at ~   ～에서 왼쪽 (오른쪽)으로 도십시오

○ You'll find it on your right   당신의 오른쪽에 있습니다.

○ My pleasure   = It's my pleasure. Thank you 에 대한 대답으로 You're welcome 과 같다.

8 손님에게 주차 안내

A How may I help you?

B Could you validate my parking ticket?

A Definitely.

B It was really hard to find a parking spot today.
What was worse, I was not allowed to park on the ground level.

A Ah, we're sorry. Our parking lot is very limited. When you can not find a parking spot, you can use the public parking lot next to this building. You can get three hours of free parking.

B Oh, I see. Thanks.

⟳ Could you validate my parking ticket?   주차권 확인 좀 해 주시겠어요?

⟳ Definitely   전적으로 동의하거나 강하게 긍정 할 때. Certainly의 의미이다.

⟳ Parking spot   주차 공간 (주차할 자리)

⟳ What was worse   게다가 심지어, 설상가상으로

⟳ Ground level   지상층, 1층 (Basement level : 지하층)

⟳ Public parking lot   공공 주차장

1. How far is it?

➡ 얼마나 멀어요?

2. It's not so far.   별로 안 멀어요.

      quite close.   꽤 가까워요.

      a long way to walk.   걷기엔 좀 멀어요.

      about one kilometer from here.   여기서 1km 쯤 되요.

3. _____A_____ is approximately 10 minutes _____B_____ from _____C_____

                                       (walk / by taxi)

➡ A는 B(수단)로 C에서 약 10분 거리입니다.

4. You're going the wrong way.

➡ 길을 잘못 가고 계시군요.

5. Come out of _____A_____ and you will see _____B_____ straight ahead of you and to the right (left) _____C_____ .

➡ A 에서 나오면 바로 앞쪽으로 B가 보이고, 오른쪽(왼쪽)으로는 C가 보입니다.

6. You will see _____A_____ on the right, and _____B_____ on the left.

➡ 오른쪽으로는 A가 보이고, 왼쪽으로는 B가 보일 것입니다.

7. Head towards _____A_____ and you will see _____B_____ .

➡ A를 향해서 가면 B가 보일 것입니다.

8. After you pass _____A_____ , turn right onto 5th Avenue.

➡ A를 지나서 오른쪽으로 돌아 5번가로 들어서세요.

9. Go to _____A_____ and cross (but don't cross) it.

➡ A로 가서 그것을 건너세요. (A까지 가되 건너지는 마세요)

10. Go straight along _____A_____ until you come to _____B_____ .

➡ B 도달할 때까지 A를 따라 쭉 가세요.

11. Before you reach _____A_____, you will pass _____B_____ on your right.

➡ A에 도달하기 전에, 오른쪽으로 B를 지나게 됩니다.

12. You'll pass _____A_____ on your left.

➡ 왼쪽으로는 A를 지나쳐 가게 될겁니다.

13. Take _____A_____ to _____B_____.

➡ A를 타고 B로 가세요.

14. Get off at _____A_____, then transfer to _____B_____.

➡ A에서 내려서 B로 갈아 타세요.

15. Take exit number 1.

➡ 1번 출구로 나가세요.

16. Go straight along ~

➡ ~을 따라 쭉 가세요.

17. Continue straight on past some traffic lights.

➡ 신호등 몇 개 지나고 쭉 가세요.

18. Continue straight ahead for about 500 meters.

➡ 500미터쯤 쭉 가세요.

19. Turn to the right (left). / Make a right (left) turn.

➡ 오른쪽(왼쪽)으로 도세요.

20. It's opposite (next to, behind, before) ~

➡ 그것은 ~반대편에 (옆에, 뒤에, 전에) 있습니다.

21. It's on your right (left). / It's on your right (left) hand side.

➡ 당신 오른 쪽 (왼쪽)에 있습니다.

A   Excuse me, how can I get to the museum?

B   Go straight along the 1st Avenue, and turn right on Washington Street.
Then, go straight two blocks. You'll find the museum on your right.

A   How far is it?

B   It's not so far.

BUSINESS
ENGLiiSH for
SECRETARIES

Making Reservations

Making Reservations

최근에는 우리 나라에서도 각종 서비스를 이용하려면 예약은 필수이다. 호텔, 비행기, 식당 등을 예약하거나 예약을 변경하는 표현을 익혀 둔다. 예약을 하기 위해 항공사, 호텔, 식당과 직접 영어로 대화할 일도 있겠지만, 비서로써 상사의 일정을 관리하고, 출장을 준비하는 과정에서 상사와의 예약 관련 대화도 필수이다.

1 호텔 예약하기

> **A** Good morning, Regent Hotel. How may I help you?
>
> **B** I'd like to book a single room from May 1st to 3rd.
>
> **A** May I ask your name, please?
>
> **B** My name is Jihyun Hwang from Jinil Company, and I'd like to make a reservation under the name of Mr. Scott Marley.
>
> **A** Can you spell his name, please?
>
> **B** Sure. S-C-O-T-T is his first name and the last name is M-A-R-L-E-Y.
>
> **A** We'll reserve a single room from May 1st to 3rd under the name of Mr. Scott Marley. Thank you for calling.
>
> **B** May I ask your name please?

- ⏻ **make a reservation** 예약하다. =book, reserve
- ⏻ **single room** 1인실 (single 침대가 하나 있는 방)

  double room 2인실 (double 침대가 하나 있는 방)

  twin room 2인실 (single 침대가 두 개 있는 방)

  suite 작은 응접실이 딸린 방

  adjoining room 연결되어 있는 방
- ⏻ **first name** 이름

  last name 성

  middle name 중간 이름 (있는 경우)
- ⏻ **May I ask your name, please?** 예약할 때는 예약 받은 담당자 이름을 적어 놓는 것이 좋다.

A   Good morning, Reservations. How can I help you?

B   Hello. I'd like to book a room. Do you have a room with a double bed for next Thursday, the 23rd?

A   How long will you be staying?

B   I'll be staying for two nights from Thursday to Saturday.

A   We have a room with a double bed for those dates.

B   Good. What's the rate for the room?

A   A double room starts from 250 dollars per night.

 What's the rate for the room?   방값이 얼마입니까?

  = What's the room rate?

⏻ per   ~당   per night   일박당

A   Intercontinental Hotel. How may I direct your call?

B   Reservations, please.

A   Just a moment, please.

C   Reservations. How may I help you?

A   I'd like to make a reservation. Do you have a double room available from the 15th of March through the 17th?

C   Yes, we have.

     ……...

     Your room is booked from March 15th to 17th.

     May I have your credit card number to guarantee your reservation?

A   It's 1234-5678-1100-1200

Business English for Secretaries

○ How may I direct your call?   어디로 연결해 드릴까요?

○ May I have your credit card number to guarantee your reservation?   예약을 보증하기 위해 신용카드 번호를 알려 주시겠습니까?

A   Reservations. May I help you?

B   I'd like to book a room for the 16th of May.

A   How long are you going to stay?

B   Check-in would be on May 16th and check-out would be on 18th.

A   What kind of room would you like?

B   I'd like a junior suite.

A   I'm sorry but the only room available at the moment is a room with a queen-sized bed.

B   Then I'll take it.

How long are you going to stay?   얼마나 묵으실 겁니까?

2   호텔 예약 취소하기

A	Reservations. How can I help you?
B	I'd like to cancel the room reserved for March 24th.
A	What name is it under?
B	Sooji Park.
A	Okay. We will cancel your reservation minus a cancellation fee of $100, and issue a refund in the amount of $300.
B	Thank you.

⏻ cancel   취소하다.

⏻ What name is it under?   어느 분 이름으로 되어있죠?

⏻ cancellation fee   취소 수수료

⏻ issue a refund   환불해주다

Business English for Secretaries

A   Good afternoon. May I help you?

B   I'd like to check in, please.

A   Do you have a reservation, sir?

B   Yes. My name is Daniel Ahn and I have a reservation for two nights.

A   Mr. Ahn, we've reserved a double room for you.
Can I have your passport and a credit card?

B   Here you are.

A   Thank you. Your room number is 556. It's on the fifth floor.
Complimentary breakfast is served at Sunrise Café on the first floor from 7 a.m. till 10 a.m.
If you have any questions or requests, please dial "0" from your room.

○ check in   입실 수속
    check out   퇴실 수속
○ I have a reservation.   예약을 해 두었습니다.
○ passport   여권
○ complimentary breakfast   무료 조식

참고

Hotel 관련 용어

- **valet parking**　주차 대행 서비스
- **lobby**　로비
- **luggage cart**　짐수레
- **front desk**　프런트 데스크
- **guest room**　객실
- **room service**　룸서비스
- **mini bar**　호텔 객실의 냉장고에 유료로 술, 음료수, 안주류 등을 갖추어 놓은 것
- **laundry**　세탁
- **housekeeping**　청소를 해 주고 요청시 필요 물품들을 가져다 줌
- **ballroom**　연회장
- **conference room**　대회의실
- **concierge**　투숙객의 편의를 위해 관광 안내나 교통편 안내 등을 함
- **air-conditioning**　에어컨 시설
- **business center**　투숙객의 사무를 위해 팩스, 인터넷 등을 서비스하는 곳
- **fitness center**　운동 시설
- **accommodation**　숙박
- **airport shuttle**　공항 셔틀 버스
- **complimentary**　무료의
- **amenities**　(호텔에 갖춰져 있는) 설비

4 비행기표 예약과 변경

비행기표 예약하기

A   I'd like to reserve a plane ticket to Milan on Feb. 3.

B   On Feb. 3, there's a flight leaving at 4 p.m.

A   Isn't there any earlier flight?

B   I'm afraid not, sir.

A   Then I'll take it.

B   Business class or economy class?

A   I want to travel in economy class. And I'd like to get an open-ended return ticket, please.

B   Sure. Please wait a moment, sir. I'll check it for you.

⏻ plane ticket   비행기표

⏻ economy class   이코노미 클래스

business class   비즈니스 클래스, prestige class 라고도 한다.

first class   일등석

⏻ open-ended ticket   돌아오는 날짜를 정하지 않은 비행기표로 대개 open ticket이라고 한다.

⏻ one-way ticket   편도표

⏻ round-trip ticket   왕복표

A	Delta Airlines. May I help you?
B	I'd like to book a round trip flight to New York.
A	Yes, ma'am. When would you like to leave?
B	The 5th of the following month.
A	All right. We have a flight leaving on the 5th at 1 p.m. Shall I book you on that, ma'am?
B	Yes, please.
A	O.K. And when would you like to return?
B	The 10th of the same month.
A	We have two flights available on that day, one at 11 a.m. and the other at 7 p.m. Which flight do you prefer?
B	I'll take the 7 p.m. flight.

book a flight / reserve a flight   비행기를 예약하다

the following month   다음 달

Shall I book you on that?   그것을 예약해 드릴까요?

on that day   그 날

A   I'd like to book a flight to Tokyo on the 24th of December.

B   There are no vacant seats.

A   Then can you find me a seat on the 23rd or the 25th instead?

B   I'm sorry. Every flight is fully booked.

A   Can you place my name on the waiting list, then?

B   May I have your name please?

A   John Kim.

fully booked   예약 완료되었습니다. = booked out

vacant seat   빈 좌석

Can you place my name on the waiting list?   대기자 명단에 이름을 올려주시겠습니까?

비행기표 예약 변경

A I'd like to change my reservation.

B May I have your name and flight number?

A My name is Julie Dorsey and flight number is CP305.

B How do you want your reservation changed?

A I'd like to cancel my reservation for the flight on January 10th, and book one on February 10th instead, please.

B All right. Let me check if there are any seats available······
We have a few open seats on the 7 p.m. flight.

A Great. Please book me for the 7 p.m. flight.

B O.K. ma'am, your reservation has been changed from CP305 to CP 307 departing Incheon at 7 p.m. and arriving in Hong Kong at 9 p.m. local time.

- How do you want your reservation changed? 예약을 어떻게 바꾸고 싶으세요?
- cancel the reservation 예약을 취소하다.
- depart 출발하다
- local time 현지 시각

On-line Reservation

요즘은 항공권 예약이 많은 경우 온라인으로 진행된다.
좌석 배치도(seat map)를 통해 좌석 지정도 가능하다.

Standard Reservation ☐ Award Reservation ☐

Round trip ☐ One-way ☐

From (a departure point) _____ To (an arrival point) _____

Depart date _____ Return date _____

Cabin Class (First ☐ Prestige or Business ☐ Premium Economy ☐ Economy ☐)

Passenger (Adult ☐ Child ☐ Infant ☐)

Online 예약 티켓에 대한 변경 문의

A How can I make changes to the booking I made online?

B Please. Log on to the system and go to the "Manage Booking".
If your booking is eligible for online changes, a link to "Change Booking" will be shown.

A Thanks.

B By the way, depending on the terms associated with your purchased fare, change may not be allowed. Or penalties might apply depending on the fare conditions.

A I see. If I have further questions, I'll call this number again.

B Sure. Thank you for calling ABC airlines.

○ eligible   (자격 · 연령 등의 조건이 맞아서) ···을 가질[할] 수 있는

○ depending on   ～에 따라

○ terms   조건

○ fare   (교통) 요금

○ fare conditions   가격 조건

○ If I have further questions   질문이 더 있으면

Business English for Secretaries

A   I'd like to book a table for five people at 7 o'clock on Saturday the 22nd of May, please.

B   I'm afraid we're fully booked on Saturday the 22nd. But we have a table on the 21st.

A   OK. Friday the 21st is fine.

B   So, that's a table for five at 7 on Friday the 21st of May.

A   That's right.

B   May I have your name, sir?

A   Roger. R-O-G-E-R.

B   Mr. Roger, we look forward to seeing you on Friday the 21st of May. Have a good day.

⏻ Saturday the 22nd of May. 또는 Saturday, May 22nd로 표기한다.

⏻ fully booked   예약이 꽉 차 있습니다.

A   Good morning. Chelsea Restaurant. May I help you?

B   I'd like to reserve a table for Friday evening.

A   All right. What time will it be, ma'am?

B   Around six.

A   Certainly. How many people are there in your party?

B   Five people.

A   Do you have any table preference?

B   We'd like to have a table in a quiet corner.

A   What name shall I put the reservation under?

B   Tina Fay.

A   Sure. A table for five is reserved for Friday six o'clock under the name of Tina Fay.

B   Thank you.

⏻ What time will it be?   몇 시가 될까요?

⏻ How many people are there in your party?   일행이 몇 분인가요?

⏻ table preference   선호하는 테이블 (선호하는 자리)

⏻ What name shall I put the reservation under?   어느 분 성함으로 예약해 드릴까요?

예약 지시 받기 > 예약 하기 > 예약 상황 보고하기

비행기 · 호텔 예약 지시

A : Dave Park   **B :** secretary

> **A** I have a business trip to Tokyo next Tuesday morning.
> Please make a hotel and flight reservation for me.
>
> **B** You leave on April 3rd?
>
> **A** Yes. I have to arrive at Haneda airport no later than noon.
>
> **B** When do you expect to be back?
>
> **A** On April 6th. I have a meeting at 10 a.m. on that day.
> Please book me on the late afternoon flight. Around 5 p.m.
>
> **B** Shall I reserve a room at the Hyatt Hotel?
>
> **A** That's good. Thanks.

☼ **no later than ~** : 늦어도 ~ 까지는

☼ 비행기 예약시 선호 좌석 (seating preference)를 확인할 수 있다.

Do you have any seat preference?

Yes, I'd like an aisle seat.

Aisle seat 통로쪽 좌석   **Window seat** 창문쪽 좌석

여행사 직원을 통해 상사의 비행기표, 호텔 예약

A : travel agent   B : secretary

A   Good morning. Ace travel. How may I help you?

B   I'd like to reserve a round-trip business class ticket to Tokyo
     under the name of Mr. Dave Park.
     He will leave Incheon on April 3rd at around 9 a.m. and fly back
     on April 6th at around 5 p.m.

A   Let me check … Some seats are available on Korean Air.
     On April 3rd.... some seats are available on 9 a.m. flight.
     And on April 6th, just one business seat is available on 5:30 p.m.
     flight.

B   That's good.

A   Could you scan the data page of his passport and send it through
     email?

B   I'll do that right now. Thank you.
     And one more thing, please make a reservation for a double
     room at the Hyatt Hotel during that period.

B   Definitely. I'll phone you as soon as everything is set.
     (After 2~3 hours)

A   I emailed you your boss's reservation confirmation. Payment
     should be completed by March 28th. E-ticket itinerary and
     receipt will be emailed after the payment.

B   Thank you.

A   Room reservation is also confirmed and you will receive a
     confirmation email from the Hyatt Hotel.

Business English for Secretaries

- ⏻ under the name of ~ : ~ 이름으로
- ⏻ data page of his passport (data page at the passport's inner cover)   여권 커버 안쪽에 여권번호, 이름, 국적, 발행일, 기간만료일 등이 나와있는 페이지.
- ⏻ And one more thing   그리고 한 가지 더
- ⏻ everything is set   모든 것이 준비되다. 모든 것이 완결되다
- ⏻ reservation confirmation   예약확인
- ⏻ e-ticket itinerary and receipt   전자항공권, 전자항공권 발행 확인서

예약 상황 보고

A : Secretary   **B** : Dave Park

> **A**   Mr. Park, your round-trip business class ticket is confirmed.
> You are booked on the 9 a.m. flight on April 3rd and the 5:30 p.m. flight on April 6th. I also received confirmation email from the Hyatt Hotel.
> Let me give you your e-ticket and hotel reservation confirmation as soon as payment is completed.
>
> **B**   Thanks.

8 예약 변경 보고

비행기표 변경 지시 > 변경 > 보고

예약 변경 지시

A : Mr. Brian Woods   B : Secretary

> A   Unexpectedly, I have to stay at Pusan longer.
>   Please cancel 5:30 p.m. flight and book me on the last flight.
>
> B   I'll do that right away.

예약 변경

A : Secretary   B : Airline reservation agent

> A   I'd like to change a reservation under the name of Brian Woods.
>   He's booked to fly back to Seoul at 5:30 p.m.
>
> B   How do you want it changed?
>
> A   What time does the last flight for Seoul leave?

B	The last flight leaves at 9:30 p.m.
	We have only one business class seat available. Shall I make a reservation?
A	No seats left in the economy class?
B	We're sorry. It's a peak season and every economy seat is fully booked.
A	Okay. Then, I will take it.

⏻ fly back to Seoul   (비행기로) 서울로 돌아오다.

⏻ the last flight for Seoul   서울행 마지막 비행기

⏻ Peak season   성수기 (busy season, high season)

　Off season   비수기 (low season)

예약 변경 보고

A : Mr. Brian Woods   B : Secretary

A	Hello, Miss Kim?
B	Yes. I changed your reservation to 9:30 flight.
	You are booked on a business class seat because it is the only seat available.

9 식당 예약 보고

상사의 식당 예약 지시 > 예약 > 예약상황 보고

예약 지시

A : Steve McKean   B : Secretary

A	I have an important business luncheon tomorrow at noon with executive directors of KM Electronics. Please reserve a table for five.
B	Yes, Mr. McKean. Do you have a specific restaurant in mind?
A	Hana Sushi or Sushi Nami would be good. Hana Sushi would be preferable.
B	All right. I'll find out if I can book a private dining room at Hana Sushi first.

- business luncheon   비즈니스 오찬
- executive director (기업체의) 전무[상무] (이사)
- private dining room (PDR)
  식당에서 식사를 겸해 사교와 비즈니스에 적합하도록 독립된 개별 공간
- preferable   더 좋은, 선호되는

Business English for Secretaries

예약

A : Restaurant staff   B : Secretary

A	Good morning. Hana Sushi. How may I help you?
B	I'd like to reserve a private dining room for 5 tomorrow at noon.
A	Wait a second, let me check....... We have one available.
B	Please put the reservation under the name of Steve Mckean.
A	Very good, ma'am.

⏻ **very good**   좋습니다. 알았습니다.

예약 상황 보고

Mr. McKean. I reserved a private dining room for five at Hana Sushi under your name.

비행기 예약 관련 용어

⬆ E-Ticket Itinerary & Receipt   예약번호(booking reference), 승객 이름, 편명, 좌석 등급, 탑승일, 탑승구, 출발/도착시간, 좌석번호(지정한 경우), 현지 연락처 등의 정보가 자세히 기재되어 있다.

⬆ round-trip ticket   왕복 티켓
  one-way ticket   편도 티켓

⬆ earlier flight / later flight
  first flight / next flight / last flight
  morning flight / afternoon flight / evening flight / night flight

⬆ economy class / business class / first class

⬆ frequent flier miles = frequent flier points = air miles = mileage

⬆ off season(low season)   비수기
  busy season(peak season)   성수기

The Royal Hotel

Reservation Confirmation

Dear Ms. Kim,

Thank you for choosing to stay with us at the Royal Hotel. We are pleased to confirm your reservation and look forward to your visit. Please review this information carefully to ensure your understanding is the same as ours.

Confirmation Number:	RH1234
Guest Name:	Ms. Ally Kim
Arrival Date:	April 10, 2015
Departure Date:	April 12, 2015
Number of Guests:	2
Room Type:	Mountain View Suite
Rate per Night:	$200.00
Check-in Time:	2:00 P.M.
Check-out Time:	11:00 A.M.

Should you require an early check-in or late check-out, please make your request as soon as possible. If you need to cancel your reservation, the Royal Hotel requires at least a 24 hour advance notification to avoid a charge for one night's room rate. If you have any questions, or need further information, call us at 800-100-1234 or click Reservations here.

We look forward to welcoming you to the Royal Hotel.

Sincerely,

David Park
Reservations Department

E-ticket

비행기 티켓을 예약하면 먼저 항공 예약 상황을 (reservation status) 이메일로 받고, 그 이후 정해진 기한 내에 요금을 내고 발권을 하게 되면 E-Ticket 을 받게 된다. E-ticket 은 ITR (Itinerary & Receipt) 이라고도 하는데 비행기표와 영수증의 역할을 하게된다. 공항에 따라서는 복사본을 요구할 수 있으니 상사가 출장을 가게 될 때 반드시 인쇄본을 준비해서 전달한다.

a. Reservation Status

비행편명 : KO 085

출발지	서울(ICN) INCHEON INTERNATIONAL	출발시간	2015년 04월 13일(월) 19시30분
도착지	뉴욕(JFK) JOHN F KENNEDY INTL	도착시간	2015년 04월 13일(월) 21시00분
예약등급	프레스티지(Z)	좌석번호	미확정
예약상태	확 약	예약번호	8SFI29
기종	AIRBUS INDUSTRIE A380-800	예상 비행거리	11084 킬로, 6887 마일
	PASSENGER	예상 비행시간	14시간 30분

비행편명 : KO 086

출발지	뉴욕(JFK) JOHN F KENNEDY INTL	출발시간	2015년 04월 20일(월) 00시50분
도착지	서울(ICN) INCHEON INTERNATIONAL	도착시간	2015년 04월 21일(화) 04시10분
예약등급	프레스티지(Z)	좌석번호	미확정
예약상태	확 약	예약번호	8SFI29
기종	AIRBUS INDUSTRIE A380-800	예상 비행거리	11084 킬로, 6887 마일
	PASSENGER	예상 비행시간	14시간 20분

b. International Flight E-Ticket

승객성명	Passenger Name	LEE/DAVIDMR BK42378534
예약번호	Booking Reference	0641-9783
항공권번호	Ticket Number	1107947783465

여정 Itinerary

편명 Flight	KE0081 (예약번호:Z62M74) Operated by KE(KOREAN AIR)				
출발 Departure	서울(ICN) Incheon intl	05Jan15 10:05	Local Time	Terminal No. : –	
도착 Arrival	뉴욕(JFK) John f kennedy	05Jan15 10:00	Local Time	Terminal No. : 1	
예상비행시간	Flight Time	13H 55M	SKYPASS 마일리지	SKYPASS Miles	6879

예약등급	Class	B (일반석)	항공권	Not Valid	
			유효기간	— Before	
좌석 타입	Seat	—		Not Valid	05Jan16
예약상태	Type Status	OK (확약)	수하물	After Baggage	2PC
운임	Fare Basis	BHXEKA			
기종	Aircraft Type	AIRBUS INDUSTRIE A380			
		—800 PASSENGER			

편명 **KE0086** (예약번호:**Z62M74**) Operated by **KE(KOREAN AIR)**
Flight

출발	뉴욕(JFK) John f		Local	Terminal No. :
Departure 도착	kennedy	30May15 00:50	Time Local	1 Terminal No. : —
Arrival	서울(ICN) Incheon intl 31May15 04:10		Time	

예상비행시간	Flight Time	14H 20M	SKYPASS 마일리지	SKYPASS Miles	6879
예약등급	Class	M (일반석)	항공권 유효기간	Not Valid Before	—
좌석 타입	Seat	—		Not Valid	05Jan16
예약상태	Type Status	OK (확약)	수하물	After Baggage	2PC
운임	Fare Basis	MHXEKA			
기종	Aircraft Type	AIRBUS INDUSTRIE A380—			
		800 PASSENGER			

항공권 운임정보 Ticket/Fare Information

연결항공권	Conj.Ticket No.	—
운임산출내역	Fare Calculation	SEL KE NYC1357.17KE SEL1250.08NUC2607.25END ROE1027.210000 XF JFK4.5
산출운임	Fare Amount	KRW 2678200 (Paid Amount KRW 2678200)
지불화폐	Equiv. Fare Paid	
세금/항공사 부과 금액	Taxes/Carrier-imposed Fees	Paid Amount KRW 342500
* 세금	Taxes	KRW 28000BP 6100YC 19200US 19200US 5500XA 7700XY 6200AY 5000XF
* 유류할증료	Fuel Surcharge	KRW 245600YR
부가수수료	Service Fees	0
총산출금액	Total Amount	KRW 3020700 (Total Paid Amount KRW 3020700)
지불수단	Form of Payment	CCCA XXXXXXXXXXX9139 / 0618/00
발행일 발행처	e-Ticket Issue Date/Place	17Nov2014 / 17300054 / SELKP3420

* 지불금액은 (Total Paid Amount)에 표기된 금액을 확인하시기 바랍니다.

수하물 규정 안내 Baggage Information

ICNJFK
첫번째 위탁 수하물	:	FREE OF CHARGE (UPTO50LB 23KG AND62LI 158LCM)
두번째 위탁 수하물	:	FREE OF CHARGE (UPTO50LB 23KG AND62LI 158LCM)
기내 휴대 수하물 정보	:	ICNJFK Default Carry On Baggae

Link : 대한항공

JFKICN
첫번째 위탁 수하물	:	FREE OF CHARGE (UPTO50LB 23KG AND62LI 158LCM)
두번째 위탁 수하물	:	FREE OF CHARGE (UPTO50LB 23KG AND62LI 158LCM)
기내 휴대 수하물 정보	:	JFKICN Default Carry On Baggae

Link : 대한항공

LB = 파운드, KG = 킬로그램, LI = 인치, LCM = 센티미터

c. Domestic Flight E-ticket

승객성명
Passenger Name
    KIM/GRACEMS
    BK64353443
예약번호
Booking Reference
    1023-9685
항공권번호
Ticket Number
    1937751156968

여정 Itinerary

			Itinerary			
편명 Flight	KE1215 Operated by KE1215					
출발 Departure	서울(GMP) Gimpo		08Apr15	10:05 Local Time	Terminal No. : D	
도착 Arrival	제주(CJU) Jeju		08Apr15	11:10 Local Time	Terminal No. : -	

			Itinerary		
예상시간	Flight Duration	01H 05M	SKYPASS 마일리지	SKYPASS Miles	276
예약등급	Class	Y (일반석)	항공권 유효기간	Not Valid Before	30Mar15
예약상태	Status	OK (확약)		Not Valid After	30Mar16
운임	Fare Basis	YLX	수하물	Baggage	20K
좌석번호	Seat No.	42B			
기종	Aircraft Type	BOEING 737-900			

			Itinerary			
편명 Flight	KE1222 Operated by KE1222					
출발 Departure	제주(CJU) Jeju	10Apr15		12:55 Local Time	Terminal No. : -	
도착 Arrival	서울(GMP) Gimpo	10Apr15		14:00 Local Time	Terminal No. : D	

			Itinerary		
예상시간	Flight Duration	01H 05M	SKYPASS 마일리지	SKYPASS Miles	276
예약등급	Class	Y (일반석)	항공권 유효기간	Not Valid Before	30Mar15
예약상태	Status	OK (확약)		Not Valid After	30Mar16
운임	Fare Basis	YLW5	수하물	Baggage	20K
좌석번호	Seat No.	30D			
기종	Aircraft Type	BOEING 737-900			

항공권 운임정보 Ticket/Fare Information

		information
연결 항공권	Conj.Ticket No.	-
운임 산출내역	Fare Calculation	SEL KE CJU82000KE SEL95000KRW177000END
산출 운임	Fare Amount	KRW 177000 (Paid Amount KRW 177000)
지불 화폐	Equiv. Fare Paid	
세금/항공사 부과 금액	Taxes/Carrier Imposed Fees	KRW 12400
* 세금	Tax	KRW 8000DA
* 유류할증료	Fuel Surcharge	KRW 4400YR
총 산출금액	Total Amount	KRW 189400
실제 지불금액	Total Paid Amount	(Total Paid Amount KRW 189400)
지불 수단	Form of Payment	CCCA XXXXXXXXXXX0939 / 0918/00
발행일 발행처	Ticket Issue Date/Place	30Mar2015 / 17326654 / SELK131KA

Business English for Secretaries

BUSINESS
ENGLiISH for
SECRETARIES

Office Works & Computer / Machine Problems

Office Works & Computer / Machine Problems

사무실에서 상사, 동료들과 생활하면서 필요한 각종 생활 영어를 익힌다. 사무실 비품의 위치를 묻거나 지시를 받고 도움을 요청할 때의 표현과 문서작성, 기계, 컴퓨터 관련 용어와 필수 표현을 익혀 둔다.

참고

지시 사항 관련 표현

Fill in the blank It is (GDP).	Circle the answer GDP or GNP	Mark the answer sheet 1) A ○ B ○ C ○ D ●
Cross out the word GDP GNP GNI	Underline the word GDP GNP GNI	Put the words in order it, the, value, market, is It is the market value.
Match the items GDP – gross domestic product GNP – gross national product	Check your work GDP G-D-P	Correct the mistake GMP – GNP

- **brainstorm a list**   머리를 짜서 목록을 만들다.
- **discuss the list**   목록에 관해 토의하다.
- **write a first draft**   초안을 작성하다.
- **edit the paper**   문서를 수정하다.
- **rewrite the paper**   문서를 다시 쓰다.
- **get feedback**   피드백을 받다.
- **turn in the paper**   문서를 제출하다.

1 사무실 비품 관련 문의

A   Do you know where the files are?

B   Why don't you check the file cabinet? They should be there.

○ **Why don't you ~**   ∼ 를 해 보지 않겠습니까? (제안)

A   Excuse me. Where can I find papers?

B   Papers? They're in the supply room.

A   I'm sorry. Did you say the supply room?

B   Yes. The supply room is on the second floor.

A   Thanks very much.

○ **supply room**   비품실

A   Can I borrow this book?

B   Sure. Go ahead.

A   Can you lend me your cellular phone?

B   I'm afraid mine has run out of battery.

 borrow   (다른 사람에게서) 빌리다

  lend   (남에게 물건을) 빌려 주다

Go ahead.   그러세요

cellular phone   핸드폰. 간단히 cell phone 이라고도 하고 mobile phone이라고도 한다.

run out of battery   배터리가 다 나가다.

Office equipment 관련 용어

- **calculator** 계산기
- **copy machine / photocopier** 복사기
- **file folder** 파일을 넣는 폴더
- **supply cabinet** 비품 캐비닛
- **stacking tray** 우편물 등을 쌓아 놓는 서랍단으로 In-box(받은 우편물함)와 Out-box(보낼 우편물함)로 구별되어 있는 경우가 보통이다.
- **paper shredder** 서류 분쇄기
- **swivel chair** 회전 의자
- **stapler** 호치키스
- **staples** 호치키스 심
- **staple remover** 스테이플을 제거하는 기구
- **hole punch** 종이에 구멍을 뚫는 기구
- **rubber stamp** 고무 도장
- **memo pad** 절취식의 메모장
- **trash bin** 휴지통
- **correction fluid** (= white-out) 수정액
- **label** 라벨 (발음에 주의할 것)
- **clear tape** 투명한 테이프 (일명 스카치 테이프)
- **push pin, thumbtack** 압정
- **paper clip** 클립
- **rubber band** 고무줄
- **organizer** (스케쥴 관리하는) 수첩
- **appointment book** 약속시간을 기입해두는 수첩
- **eraser** 지우개
- **ruler** 자
- **scissors** 가위
- **highlighter** 형광펜
- **laptop** notebook 이라고 흔히 부르는 portable computer
- **beam projector** 빔 프로젝터
- **visual aids** 시각 자료

2   도움을 청하고 받기

A	Could you do me a favor?
B	Sure. What is it?
A	Can you get a sandwich for me? I don't have time to go out for lunch today.
B	Sure. What kind of sandwich do you want?
A	I'd like to have a BLT sandwich on whole wheat bread.
B	Certainly.

- **Could you do me a favor?**   (도움을 청할 때) 부탁 하나 드려도 될까요?

  = Would you do me a favor? Will you do me a favor? May I ask you a favor?

- **Can you get ~ for me?**   ~을 저에게 가져다 주겠어요?

- **BLT sandwich**   Bacon, lettuce and Tomato sandwich

- **whole wheat bread**   통밀빵   **white bread**   흰 빵

A   Mr. Martin, is there anything I can do for you?

B   Can you order a taxi, please?

A   Yes, sir. I'll order you one now.

Is there anything I can do for you?　　도움 줄 일이 없는지를 물어 볼 때.

= Would you like me to-?

= If you need any help, just let me know.

Can you order a taxi?　　택시를 불러 주겠어요?

A   Can you help me analyze these numbers?
     I am not good at data handling on computer.

B   Sure. I'm pretty familiar with the job. Let me know if you need
     help with anything.

---

analyze   분석하다

3 문서 작성 요청

> A Would you do me a favor?
>
> B Sure. What is it?
>
> A Could you print out ten copies of this document?
>   I have it saved on a network share.
>
> B I'll take care of it right away.

 document   서류

 I'll take care of it right away   바로 해 드리겠습니다.

A   I need your assistance.

       Could you please finish this report by 5 o'clock?

B   I'm sorry, but I have to handle this paperwork first.

       Can it wait?

A   No, it can't wait.

- assistance   도움
- Can it wait?   나중에 해도 되는 일인가요?

  Should I do it now? 또는 Can I do it later? 라고 말할 수도 있다.
- handle ~ first   ~을 먼저 처리하다.
- paperwork   서류작업

A   I am due to give a presentation on our new fingerprint sensor next Monday.
    Could you please help me prepare the presentation?

B   Sure. I'd be happy to.

A   Create PowerPoint slides, please.
    And could you please apply animation effects on a slide-by-slide basis?

B   Yes, I will.
    Until when do I have to create it?

A   At least until this Friday.

🔾 **be due to**   ～하기로 (예정)되어있다.

🔾 **give a presentation**   발표하다.

🔾 **fingerprint sensor**   지문인식기

🔾 **I'd be happy to. = I would be happy to.**   기꺼이 그러겠습니다.

🔾 **animation effect**   애니메이션 효과

🔾 **on a slide-by-slide basis**   각 슬라이드 마다

A   Mr. Parker requested a copy of minutes for the board meeting.

Please send it in Microsoft Word or PDF file to his new email address.

Hangul software is not installed on his computer.

B   I'll get right on it.

- ⏻ **minutes**   회의록 (발음에 유의)
- ⏻ **board meeting**   이사회 회의
- ⏻ **PDF file**   Portable Document Format file 원래 문서의 포맷 및 기능을 그대로 보여 준다.
- ⏻ **install**   (컴퓨터 등에서 프로그램을) 깔다.
- ⏻ **I'll get right on it.**   당장 그렇게 하겠습니다.

A　We have a very important meeting tomorrow. Have you prepared our presentation materials?

B　I've almost finished. But I need to make some adjustment.
I think it'll be done in time for the meeting.

A　Be sure to have it ready by five this afternoon.
We have to review it.

B　Yes, I will.

⏻ **presentation materials**　발표자료

⏻ **adjustment**　조정, 수정

⏻ **in time**　제시간에, 늦지 않고

⏻ **be done in time for ~**　~에 늦지 않도록 시간 맞춰 끝나다

⏻ **have it ready**　준비되도록 하다.

> A This is a five-page handout for annual staff meeting. Could you please make ten copies of it?
>
> B Yes. Anything else?
>
> A We are going to have a social time with light refreshments after the meeting.
>
> B I see.

- annual staff meeting 연례 직원 회의
- make a copy 복사하다.
- social time 친목 도모를 위한 시간
- refreshments 다과

A   Could you please type up this minutes by noon?

B   Yes, I will.

A   Can you finish it in time?

B   Yes, I think I can.

A   Please make no typos.

When you complete it, please email it to all department managers.

Can you finish it in time?   제 시간 안에 끝낼 수 있으시겠어요.

typo   오타

A   Can you help me prepare the conference?

B   I'm sorry, but I'm behind in my work.

I have to submit this pre-budget report for approval by noon.

And then, I have to complete business trip report no later than 3 p.m. today.

Can I do it later?

A   Sure. It's nothing urgent.

⏻ I'm behind in my work   일이 밀렸습니다.

⏻ submit   제출하다.

⏻ pre-budget report   사전 예산 보고서

⏻ approval   승인, 결재

⏻ and then   그리고 나서

⏻ business trip report   출장 보고서

⏻ no later than   ~까지는

⏻ It's nothing urgent.   급한 일은 아닙니다.

A　When do you expect to complete the report?

B　It is about 70% done. But it will take me another one or two hours to complete it.

A　Can you meet the deadline?

B　Certainly. I'll try to complete it by this afternoon at the latest.

It is about 70% done　70% 정도 되었습니다.

It is (almost) half done　(거의) 절반 정도 되었습니다.

Can you meet the deadline?　마감기한을 맞출 수 있습니까?

at the latest　(아무리) 늦어도

at the earliest　빨라도

(ex. I can finish it in two hours at the earliest. 빨라도 2시간 후에나 끝낼 수 있다)

⬆ So far it is going well.　(So far things are going well.) 지금 까지는 잘 되고 있습니다.

⬆ Everything is on the right track.　모든 것이 제대로 되고 있습니다.

⬆ It will be done by 3 p.m. (at the latest).　(늦어도) 오후 3시까지는 다 될 겁니다.

⬆ I will get it done by tomorrow.　내일까지 끝내 놓겠습니다.

⬆ It will be done in time for the deadline.　마감시한까지 다 될겁니다.

⬆ It is almost done.　거의 다 됐습니다.

⬆ It is half done.　절반 되었습니다.

⬆ It is 70% done.　70% 되었습니다.

참고

지시 사항이 충분치 않을 때

- Could you tell me some more about that?

- Can you give me some more details about that?

- I'd like to have some more information about that.

- Can you be more specific?

- Could you elaborate (on ___)?

4 일정관리

A   What's my schedule today?

B   You have a full schedule today. It's going to be a busy day.

A   What should I do first?

B   Please handle this report first.

A   How about staff meeting?

B   That can wait.

Business English for Secretaries

⏻ **You have a full schedule today.**   오늘 일정이 꽉 차있습니다

⏻ **Please handle this report first.**   이 보고서부터 먼저 처리하는 것이 좋겠습니다.

⏻ **That can wait**   그건 나중에 해도 됩니다

A Ms. Lee, can you tell me what my schedule is today?

B You have a meeting with Robert Brown of Pacific Holdings at 10 a.m. and a luncheon appointment with the Chairman of AMCHAM at the Shilla Hotel at noon.

A Anything else?

B Mr. Johnson of Central Bank is supposed to be here at 3 p.m.

holdings 지주회사

AMCHAM (the American Chamber of Commerce in Korea) 주한 미국 상공회의소

be supposed to ～하기로 되어있다.

A   When is the stockholder's meeting scheduled?

B   It is scheduled next Monday at ten.

A   I see. I need a computer connected to a projector at the meeting.

B   I'll have it ready.

stockholder's meeting   주주총회

I'll have it ready   준비해 놓겠습니다.

> A   I have an appointment with Mr. Lee tomorrow.
>   Did you contact Mr. Lee?
>
> B   Yes, I received an email confirmation from his secretary.
>   He's due at ten tomorrow.

○ **I received an email confirmation**   이메일로 확답 받았습니다.

○ **He's due at ten tomorrow**   내일 10시에 오기로 되어있다.

회의실 잡기

> A   I need a large conference room for the afternoon of February 7th
>   and 8th.
>
> B   For how many hours do you need it, and for how many people?
>
> A   It's for 20 people, from 2 to 6 p.m.
>
> B   I'll arrange our conference room 101.

○ **conference room**   회의실

○ **arrange**   정하다. 준비하다.

손님 맞이

A　Our biggest client, Mr. Chris Ronalds is due at Incheon in two hours.

B　I've already sent a company car to pick him up.

A　Have you told the driver to take him straight to the Hilton Hotel?

B　Yes, I have.

A　And could you please confirm our reservation for a table at La Seine?

B　I've already done it.

ⓘ our biggest client　우리의 최대 고객

ⓘ be due to ~　~ 하기로 되어있다.
　　도착 예정임을 나타낼 때는 to 이하가 생략되기도 한다.

ⓘ pick up　(차, 배 등이) 도중에 태우다. (차로 사람을) 마중 나가다.

ⓘ take　~을 데리고 가다. (차 따위에) 태워가다.

ⓘ confirm　확인하다

ⓘ I've already done it.　제가 이미 했습니다.

Business English for Secretaries

출장 준비 ⟿⟿⟿⟿⟿⟿⟿⟿⟿⟿⟿⟿⟿⟿⟿⟿ ◯

A　On the 5th of next month I'll attend APE Meeting in Kuala Lumpur.
　　Could you please make my flight reservation?

B　Yes, Mr. Turner. What time does the meeting start on the 5th?

A　At 2 p.m.
　　And would you please make a return flight reservation on the 8th?

B　Yes, I will.

💡

🕛 make a return flight reservation　돌아오는 비행기편을 예약하다.

A   Could you tell me how you've planned my business trip to Hong Kong next week?

B   Yes sir. You are leaving Seoul at 9 a.m. Monday and arriving in Hong Kong at 11 a.m. local time.

A   Could you tell me about my schedule for the day?

B   There will be a meeting on financial market analysis at 6 p.m. at the Head Office.

Here's your itinerary. Is it satisfactory?

⏻ market analysis   시장 분석

⏻ itinerary   여행 계획, 방문지 리스트, 여행 일정

⏻ satisfactory   만족할 만한

5  조퇴 및 휴가 요청

> A   Is it okay if I leave early? I have a terrible headache.
>
> B   Sure, go ahead. Then, who will cover for you?
>
> A   Mr. Brown will do that.

⏻ **cover for**   ~의 업무를 대신하다. 다른 사람의 업무를 잠시 대신 맡아주는 경우에 사용한다. sub for (substitute for) 라고도 할 수 있다.

> A   I'd like to take tomorrow off. Can you cover for me?
>
> B   Sorry, I am already covering for Jane Kim.

⏻ **I'd like to take tomorrow off.**   내일 쉬고 싶습니다.

⏻ **Can you cover for me?**   제 업무를 맡아 주시겠습니까?
　Could you sub for me? Would you fill in for me? 라고도 한다.

A   Excuse me from work today. I have a bad cold.
    I called Ms.Kim and asked to cover for me.

B   That's too bad. Take good care of yourself, please.
    I hope you get well soon.

Business English for Secretaries

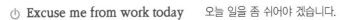

Excuse me from work today   오늘 일을 좀 쉬어야 겠습니다.

Take good care of yourself, please.   몸조리 잘 하세요.

I hope you get well soon   빨리 나으면 좋겠습니다.

get well   회복하다. 병이 낫다

참고 **휴가, 조퇴, 봉급 인상 관련 표현**

- **I'd like to take tomorrow off.** 내일 쉬고 싶습니다.

- **May I leave early?**
  Would you mind if I leave early?
  Do you think I can leave early?
  저 조퇴해도 될까요?

- **Sure, go ahead.**
  By all means.
  그러세요.
  No, I'm afraid you can't, because…
  미안하지만 좀 힘들겠네요, 왜냐하면…

- **I feel that it's about time that I had a pay rise.**
  이제 봉급을 좀 인상했으면 합니다.

- Would you mind로 물었을 경우 거절, 불허의 대답은 yes (I mind)로 하며, 허가의 대답을 no (I don't mind)로 하는 것에 유의한다.

인사 관련 용어

- **promotion**   승진
- **prospects**   (인사상의) 전망
- **recruit**   채용 공고
- **resign**   사임
- **retire**   은퇴
- **lay-off**   해고
- **salary**   임금
- **leave early**   조퇴
- **maternity leave**   출산 휴가
- **pay rise**   봉급 인상
- **compensation package**   임금과 보너스, 필요시 주택 마련에 필요한 돈 등 회사에서 직원에게 제공하는 전반적인 혜택. 자기개발 지원제도, 기숙사등의 복리 후생시설 등도 이에 해당한다.

6 | 사무실 내에서의 사교

A   Now we are going for lunch.
     Would you join us for lunch?

B   Ah, I had a large breakfast this morning and I don't feel so well.

A   Shall I get you something to eat on our way back from lunch?
     I mean, uh, porridge or something.

B   No thanks. Have a good lunch.

ⓘ **I don't feel so well**   속이 안 좋다. 몸이 안 좋다.

ⓘ **on our way back from lunch**   점심 먹고 돌아오는 길에

ⓘ **I mean**   그러니까. 그러니까 제 말은.

ⓘ **porridge or something**   죽 같은 것

7 사무 기기 고장

A	Have you finished making copies of handouts?
B	No, not yet. The copy machine is jammed again.
A	Do you know what's wrong with the printer?
B	The printer broke down.
A	The printer is out of paper. Where is the paper for the printer?
B	I'll bring some for you.

- The copy machine is jammed   복사기에 용지가 걸렸습니다.
- is wrong with ~   에 무슨 이상이 있다.
- break down   고장나다. = be out of order
- out of ~   ~ 이 없다. 떨어지다.
  out of stock   재고가 없다.

A   The coffee machine must have a problem. It is making a lot more noise and there's a lot of vibration.

B   We need to contact the company to get a service visit. As far as I know, the warranty covers the defect.

⏻ vibration   진동

⏻ service visit   서비스를 위한 방문

⏻ As far as I know   내가 아는 한

⏻ warranty   보증

⏻ defect   결점, 고장

8   컴퓨터 관련 문의 및 답변

A   I'm afraid my computer is infected with a computer virus.

B   What's wrong with your computer?

A   I cannot access the internet.

B   Why don't you download an anti-virus program and scan your computer?

A   Do you know a website for that?

B   You can use Google to search the site.

A   That's a good idea.

○ virus   컴퓨터 바이러스

○ ~ is infected with a computer virus   컴퓨터 바이러스에 감염되다.

○ access the internet   인터넷에 접속하다.

○ download a program   프로그램을 다운로드하다.

○ scan   스캔하다.

○ search the site   사이트를 검색하다.

A Could you please help me open the attached file?
   I don't know why I can't open it.

B You must install a compatible viewer.

A How can I do that?

B Viewers capable of opening this file can be found on the internet.
   Download a viewer from the internet.

○ attached file   첨부 파일
○ install   (프로그램을) 깔다.
○ viewer   편집 기능은 없지만 문서를 볼 수 있게 해 주는 프로그램.
   compatible viewer   호환가능한 뷰어

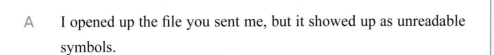

A   I opened up the file you sent me, but it showed up as unreadable symbols.

I don't know why it does that.

B   You have to open it with the right program.

ⓣ but it showed up as unreadable symbols   읽을 수 없는 기호들이 나타났다.

ⓣ open it with the right program   맞는 프로그램으로 열다.

Vocabulary for Computer

- » CPU (Central Processing Unit)   컴퓨터 본체
- » power switch   전원 스위치
- » keyboard   키보드
- » scanner   스캐너
- » laptop   노트북
- » trackball   노트북에 있는 트랙볼
- » monitor   모니터
- » junk mail   스팸 메일
- » bug   프로그램 사용 도중에 생기는 이상 현상, error
- » booting   부팅.
- » default   기본값, 표준값
- » real time   명령하자마자 실행됨
- » backup file   백업파일
- » ISP (Internet Service Provider)   인터넷 서비스업체
- » bookmark   즐겨찾기
- » URL (Uniform Resource Locator)   인터넷 정보들의 주소를 알려줌
- » USB (Universal Service Bus)   컴퓨터와 주변기기를 연결할 때 쓰이는 표준
- » drag   마우스 버튼을 누른 채 끌다
- » capture   화면에 나타난 내용을 디스크 장치에 파일로 저장하다
- » scroll   스크롤하다
- » synchronize   동기화
- » zip   압축하다
- » unzip   압축을 풀다

Vocabulary for IT
(Information Technology)

»» Adware	A software that displays advertisements such as a popup ad
»» Back up	to copy an electronic record to protect the information
»» Browser	A program or tool such as Internet Explorer or Chrome that enables you to browse internet
»» Bug	A defect or fault in a program
»» Cookies	Small pieces of information on the times and dates you have visited web sites
»» Cursor	A blinking symbol on the screen
»» Ethernet	A family of computer networking
»» Firewall	Specialized hardware or software to prevent unauthorized access to a network or computer
»» Hit	A visit to a website
»» Interface	A shared boundary across which two separate components of a computer system exchange information
»» ISP	Internet Service Provider
»» LAN	Local Area Network
»» Multitasking	Responds to input instantly
»» Open Source	A software that is freely available to be used or to be modified
»» OS	Operating System, the most important program that runs on a computer such as Android, iOS, Linux or Microsoft Windows
»» Peripheral device	A computer device that is not part of the essential computer such as key board, mouse, disk drives or printers
»» User Interface (UI)	the space where interactions between humans and machines occur
»» URL	Uniform Resource Locator, the internet address on the World Wide Web
»» Widget	A specialized application embedded in a web page

Business English for Secretaries

Privacy Policy in Enrollment Agreement

Customer's Choice to Limit Use of Data

To provide you with the opportunity to participate in offers and services which we believe would be of interest to you, where legally permitted and in accordance with our Privacy Policy, Taesung Co. may send you mailings and share personally identifiable data about you with Taesung's affiliated companies and other companies for their marketing purposes. Please read our Privacy Policy to understand our current corporate policy on privacy.

You may limit the use or disclose of personally identifiable data about you by checking one of the boxes within each of A and B below.

A. You give Taesung permission to send you marketing offers or materials and to disclose personally identifiable data about you to Taesung's affiliates for marketing purposes.
☐ 1. Postal Mail Only   ☐ 2. E-Mail Only   ☐ 3. Both Postal and E-Mail
☐ 4. You direct Taesung not to send you any marketing offers or materials and not to disclose personally identifiable data about you to Taesung's affiliates for marketing purposes.

If you do not check any of the boxes above, you will be deemed to have selected item 1.

If you check item 4, you may not receive offers and services that may be of interest to you, Taesung Award Points.

B. ☐ 1. You give Taesung permission to disclose personally identifiable data about you to companies that are not Taesung's affiliates for marketing purposes.
☐ 2. You direct Taesung not to disclose personally identifiable data about you to companies that are not Taesung's affiliates for marketing purposes.

If you do not check any of the boxes above, you will be deemed to have selected item 1.

개인정보의 보호를 위하여 개인정보 수집 및 활용 동의서의 내용을 정확히 파악하고, 동의한 범위 내에서만 자신의 개인정보를 활용하도록 규정한다. 영문으로 된 개인정보활용동의서를 읽고 그 의미를 정확히 파악하고, 개인정보 이용에 있어서 보장되어야 할 이용자의 권리를 침해받지 않도록 한다.

BUSINESS
ENGLiiSH for
SECRETARIES

Business Letter / E-mail

Business Letter / E-mail

비즈니스 레터와 이메일의 성격을 이해하고, 기본적 표현을 연습하여 어법과
상황에 적절한 서신과 이메일을 작성할 수 있도록 한다.

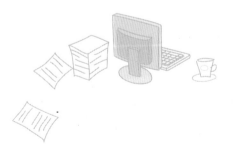

1　Business Letter

사무 서신(Business letter)은 무엇보다도 간결하고 의미가 명확하며 표현은 정중해야 한다. 영문 서신의 경우 행간 간격 없이(single-spaced) 타이핑하고 되도록이면 한 페이지 이내로 맞추는 것이 좋다. 형식, 문법, 철자, 구두점 등 세세한 부분까지 실수가 없어야 하며 오타(typo)는 절대 있어서는 안 된다. 스펠링 점검 기능(Spell checker)을 이용해 오타를 점검해야 한다.

영문 편지를 쓰는 양식 중 현재 가장 일반적인 양식은 블록 양식(Block format)으로 문장들을 왼쪽으로 정렬(left-justified)하고 문단 첫 문장이라도 들여쓰기(indent)를 하지 않는다. 또한 행간 간격이 없도록 하되 문단과 문단 사이는 한 행을 띄어(double-spaced) 쓴다.

편지의 본 내용은 1~3 문단으로 쓰는 것이 일반적이다. 감상적인 문구나 화려한 수식어는 피해서 명확한 표현을 쓴다. 받는 사람의 이름 앞에는 Mr. 나 Ms.를 붙여 정중하게 쓰는데 남성인지 여성인지를 구별하기 힘든 경우 생략할 수도 있다.

공문일 경우 편지지는 회사명과 주소가 상단에 인쇄되어 있는 (letterhead) 편지지를 쓰는 것이 일반적이다. 편지지에서 여백은 보통 위, 아래, 양 옆을 1-1.5인치 정도 둔다. 글자체(font)는 Times New Roman, 글자 크기는 12가 가장 일반적이다. 간혹 덜 정중한 개인적인 편지에서는 글자체를 Arial로 쓰는 경우가 있으나 공문의 경우 Times New Roman을 쓰는 것이 일반적이다. 편지지는 미색이나 흰색의 종이를 사용하고 검은색 잉크로 프린트하며 서명은 자필로 하며 대개 푸른색 펜을 사용한다.

대문자(capital letter)는 문법상 필요할 때에만 써야 하며 꼭 필요한 경우가 아니면 문장이나 단어 밑에 밑줄을 긋거나 진하게 쓰지 않도록 한다.

Business Letter의 구성 요소

영문 서신의 경우 아래 구성요소가 빠짐없이 들어가야 하며 아래의 순서에 맞게 들어가야 한다.

1. Letterhead / Sender's address	보내는 사람 주소
2. Date	날짜
3. Inside address	받는 사람 주소
4. Salutation / Greeting	–께, –귀하
5. Message	메시지
6. Closing / Complementary Close	끝맺음
7. Signature	서명
8. Printed name and position	보내는 사람의 이름과 직위
9. Enclosures	(필요시) 동봉물이 있음을 표시

Business Letter Structure

PanAm Company	
123 Rolling Meadows Drive	보내는 사람 주소 (미국의 경우 street address)
Ann Arbor, MI 48103	(미국의 경우 city, state zip code)
May 22, 2014	날짜
Ms. Grace Brandon	받는 사람 이름 (Mr.나 Ms.를 붙인다.)
Marketing Team	직위나 팀 (필요시)
ABC Company	회사
2453 Main Street	주소
Milan, OH 23456	
Dear Ms. Brandon:	-께 (colon : 을 사용한다.)
Introductory Paragraph:	편지를 쓰는 목적을 쓴다.
Second Paragraph:	주제를 뒷받침하는 문장 또는 추가적인 정보를 쓴다.
Concluding Paragraph:	연락처를 명기하거나 감사의 뜻을 전한다.
Sincerely,	Sincerely 뒤에는 comma ,를 쓰며 Respectfully,
	나 Truly yours,를 쓰기도 한다.
John White	3-4줄을 띄어 놓고 푸른색 펜으로 서명한다.
John White	보내는 사람 이름
CEO	필요시 직위
Enc.	동봉물(enclosure)이 있는 경우

Sample Letter 1

ACORN Tech.

135 Main Street
San Francisco, CA 13682

June 2, 2013

Hyatt Hotel
318 Wellington Street
Ann Arbor, MI 24784

Dear Sir or Madam:

I would like to request some information about your hotel. I'm planning to be in Ann Arbor on business from July 2 to July 6. Do you have a junior suite available for that period? I would also like to know what the cost would be.

Thank you in advance for your quick reply.

Sincerely yours,

Mattew Aigner

Matthew Aigner
Sales Manger
ACORN Tech.

BCD Co.

333 7th Avenue
LA, CA 24520
TEL: (533) 423 2893

Nov. 22, 2014

Meg Garrett
#202, 2763 Conwell Rd.
LA, CA 13245

Dear Ms. Garrett:

Thank you for enrolling our program. The package will be shipped November 27, 2014 and you will receive the package by November 30, 2014. We need you to review the information below.

Once you receive the package, open it up and there will be "Client Instructions" in an envelope. That will cover all the instructions that you will do to complete the program.

Last but not least, you will receive a client survey after everything has been completed. We've always tried to improve our services and find out where we've succeeded. We would appreciate it if you'd take a moment to complete it.

Please don't hesitate to call me with any questions or curiosities. Good luck with everything.

Sincerely,

Chris

Chris McDonald
Account Representative
BCD Company

BioAir Company

123 Stadium St.
Ann Arbor, MI 48103

June 1st, 2014

Ms. Susan Cunningham
Purex Inc.
2453 Main Street
Ann Arbor, MI 48103

Dear Ms. Cunningham:

We, at BioAir Company, would like to express our deepest appreciation for your continued support and to announce that we are holding a farewell party for Mr. Jason Robert, CEO of our company.

You are cordially invited to the party which will take place at Fairmont Hotel on Wednesday, June 22nd between 6 p.m. and 9 p.m. We would appreciate your R.S.V.P. to Sandy Kim at (734) 389-3243 by June 10th.

We are looking forward seeing you there.

Sincerely yours,

Laura Sullivan

Laura Sullivan
Planning Department
BioAir Company

Vocabulary

- ≫ envelope   봉투
- ≫ letter   편지
- ≫ postcard   엽서
- ≫ greeting card   축하 카드, 연하장, 인사장
- ≫ certified mail / registered mail   등기
- ≫ express mail   특급 우편
- ≫ ground post / parcel post   소포
- ≫ return address   보내는 사람 주소
- ≫ mailing address   받는 사람 주소
- ≫ invitation   초대장
- ≫ thank-you note   감사장
- ≫ letterhead paper   회사명과 주소, 전화번호 등이 상단에 인쇄되어 있는 종이

2 E-mail

비즈니스 이메일(business email)의 작성 요령은 사무 서신(business letter)의 작성 요령과 크게 다르지 않다. 영문 서신에 필요한 구성 요소들을 순서에 맞게 써 주며 정중하고 어법에 맞도록 써야 한다.

비즈니스 이메일(Business E-mail) 쓸 때 유의점

❶ 빠른 답장 (prompt response)을 한다.

❷ 적절하고 의미있게 제목을 붙인다.

❸ 정중하게 쓴다.

❹ To, From, Cc, Bcc, Reply to All 등을 적절히 쓴다.

❺ 첨부 파일을 보낼 때 첨부 파일이 빠지거나 다른 파일을 보내지 않도록 특히 유의한다.

❻ 철자, 문법에 유의한다. 스펠링 점검을 하며 보내기 전에 꼭 다시 한번 읽어 본다.

❼ 서명 블록 (Signature block)을 이용한다.

❽ 이메일에 필요한 구성 요소는 대부분 사무 서신의 구성 요소와 같다. 다만, 이메일의 경우 편지 쓴 날짜, 자필 서명이 생략되며 Dear ~ 뒤에 : (colon) 이외에도 ,(comma) 가 자주 쓰인다.

Email Structure

From:	james@cnc.com	보내는 사람
To:	mjkim@hana.co.kr	받는 사람
Cc		참조
Bcc		숨은 참조
Subject:	[Re] Inquiry about membership benefits	제목

Dear Ms. Kim,

서두 인사말
(〜씨 께)

Thank you for your inquiry about our CNC card membership. With CNC card membership, you will get the following benefits:

본문.내용

1. Cardholder-only saving events
2. Advance notice of sales
3. 10% off on everything, including food
4. No-interest financing plan
5. Free delivery service

If we can be of any assistance in the future, please call us at 800-555-3562. Thank you again for your interest.

Sincerely yours,

결구

Brenda James
Credit Card Division, CNC Department Store
30 Central Park St.
New York, NY 10114
Phone: (212) 308-1234 Fax: (212) 308-5678

사인 블럭

1 From 보내는 사람

비즈니스 이메일의 경우, 보내는 사람의 이메일 주소는 그것을 보내는 사람이 누구인지를 주소만 보고도 확연히 알 수 있도록 하는 것이 좋다. 예를 들어, 이름이 Jae-hyun Park 인 사람의 경우 jhpark@aic.com 같은 주소가 whiteangel@aic.com 류의 주소 보다 좋다.

2 To 받는 사람

모든 이메일 소프트웨어는 주소록을 작성하는 기능을 갖고 있다. 이름만 선택하면 이메일 작성 화면에 주소가 자동으로 적히게 되므로, 이를 활용하여 주소를 틀리게 쓰는 실수를 하지 않도록 한다.

3 Cc (Carbon copy) 참조.

같은 내용의 이메일을 두 사람 이상에게 보낼 때 사용한다.

4 Bcc (Blind Cc) 숨은 참조

Cc의 경우 메일을 받은 사람은 다른 누구에게도 그 메일이 갔는지 알 수 있지만, Bcc의 경우는 본인 이외에 누가 그 메일을 받았는지 알 수 없다.

5 Subject 제목

❶ 간결하면서도 제목으로 그 메일의 내용을 짐작할 수 있도록 한다.
　(바람직한 예) Board meeting on Monday
　(바람직하지 못한 예) Meeting, Hello, Thank you

❷ Subject 난이 Re: 또는 [Re]로 시작 하는 경우가 있다. 이것은 Reply to를 뜻한다. 예를 들어, subject 난이 [Re] Employment Offer로 시작하면, 이것은 Employment Offer라는 이메일에 대한 회신이 되는 것이다.

6 Greeting   서두 인사말

① 이메일 서두 인사말(greeting)의 예

Dear Mr. / Ms. + 성	Dear Mr. Willis,
Dear Mr. / Ms. + 이름 + 성	Dear Mr. Mike Wills,
Dear + 직함 + 성	Dear President Smith,
다수의 사람에게 보내는 경우	Dear staff members, All Section Chiefs:
받는 사람의 이름을 모르는 경우	To whom it may concern, Dear Sir/Madam:

② 비즈니스 이메일에서는 "Hey"나 "Hi"로 인사를 시작하는 것을 피해야 한다.

③ 서두 인사말(greeting)이 생략되는 경우도 있다.

바쁘고 빈번하게 이메일을 주고 받는 경우에는 "Dear" 로 시작하는 "~씨께"라는 서두인사말(greeting)을 생략하기도 한다. 그리고 한 가지 문제로 여러 차례 답장이 오고 가는 경우에도 처음에는 "Dear"로 시작하는 서두 인사말(greeting)을 넣더라도, 매번 이메일에서 인사말을 넣지는 않는다.

7 Message

① 예의 바르면서도 간결하고 분명하게 메시지 전달이 이루어져야 한다.

② 모든 글자를 대문자로 쓰지는 말아야 한다. 모든 글자를 대문자화(capitalize)하는 것은 소리치는(shouting) 느낌을 주며, 읽기도 쉽지 않기 때문이다.

또한 대문자가 들어가야 할 자리에까지 모두 소문자로 적는 경우에도 읽는 사람은 불편을 느끼게 된다.

③ 사안이 여러 가지인 경우 1), 2), 3) 또는 a), b), c) 와 같이 항목을 나누어 언급한다.

④ 모니터의 한 화면을 넘어가지 않도록 한다.

⑤ 장황한 표현(clutter)이나 군더더기 표현(redundancies)을 삼간다. 예를 들자면 다음과 같다.

예 장황한 표현

- a large number of → many
- at this point of time → now
- It would be highly appreciated that you → please~

예 군더더기 표현

- absolutely essential → essential
- past experience → experience
- personal opinion → opinion

❻ 내용이 길어지는 경우에는 커버 메시지(cover message)를 써서 본문은 짧게 쓰고, 첨부 파일로 보낸다.

❼ 비즈니스 이메일에서는 이모티콘 사용을 피하도록 한다. 개인적 이메일 경우 이모티콘 사용이 효과적일 수 있으나 비즈니스 이메일에서는 적절하지 않다.

8 Complementary Close 결구

다음은 비즈니스 이메일에서 실제로 많이 사용되는 결구이다.

Sincerely yours, / Sincerely, / Regards, / Best regards, / With best wishes,

9 Signature 서명

❶ 이름, 직위, 회사, 주소, 전화, 휴대전화, 팩스, 이메일, 웹사이트 링크 에 대한 정보를 넣으며, 회사명과 함께 슬로건(slogan)을 써 넣기도 한다.

❷ 길이는 5~6줄을 넘지 않도록 한다. 너무 길어지는 경우 자칫 자기중심 적인 느낌을 줄 수 있기 때문이다.

❸ 사인 블럭(sign block)을 매번 쓰는 것은 번거로운 일이므로 미리 이메일 사인 블럭을 만들어 두고 삽입한다.

❹ 가장 일반적인 형식은 다음과 같다. 경우에 따라 정보가 조금 더 추가 되거나 빠지기도 한다.

Your name typed

Your Street Address

City, State Zip Code

Telephone Number

Email Address

예 1

Jina Park

30 Central Park St.

New York, NY 10114

Phone: (212) 308-3745   Fax: (212) 308-3746

jnpark@cnc.com

예 2

Gary Morris

Overseas Marketing Manager, KARA Incorporated

Phone: (617) 954-4783   Fax: (617) 954-4782

grmorris@kara.com

예 3

Jane Kim

Senior Manager, R&D Department, Compass

123 Shinsa-dong, Kangnam-gu, Seoul, Korea 123-010

Phone: +82-2-543-0579 Fax: +82-2-543-0578

jnkim@compass.com

Changing The Way You Think About Math Education

Visit our website : http://www.compass.com/

Inbox	받은 편지함
Sent Folder / Sent	보낸 편지함
Trash Folder / Trash	휴지통
Drafts Folder / Drafts	임시 보관함
Contacts / Address book	주소록
Delete	삭제
Reply	답장하기
Forward	전달하기
@	at
.	dot

자신에 대한 소개

- I am Lisa Kim from the marketing department of JS Electronics.

  저는 JS 전자 마케팅 부서 Lisa Kim 입니다.

- My name is Jane Kim and I am in charge of overseas marketing.

  저는 Jane Kim 이며, 해외 마케팅을 담당하고 있습니다.

- This is David Kim from General Affairs Department.

  저는 총무부의 David Kim 입니다.

- This is David Kim of JS Electronics. We met at Royal Hotel last Monday.

  저는 JS전자의 David Km 입니다. 우리 지난 월요일에 Royal Hotel에서 만났었죠.

- I was referred to you by David Lee of H Tour.

  저는 H Tour의 David Lee로부터 당신을 소개(추천) 받았습니다

메일에 대한 목적 밝히기

- This is to let you know that the farewell banquet is scheduled for Tuesday evening.

  이는 송별회가 화요일 저녁에 예정되어 있음을 알리기 위함입니다.

- This is to announce several personnel changes.

  이는 몇 분의 인사 이동을 알려드리기 위함 입니다.

- I am writing to inquire about the release date of the new products.

  신상품 출시일에 대해 문의하려고 이 메일을 보냅니다.

⟨V⟩ I am writing to remind you of upcoming meeting schedule.
다가오는 미팅 스케줄을 상기시켜 드리기 위해 이 메일을 씁니다.

답장으로써 메일 쓰기

⟨V⟩ I am responding to your email dated January 15th.
1월 15일자 메일에 대해 답하겠습니다.

⟨V⟩ Here is my answer to your question of March 21st.
3일 21일자 당신 질문에 대한 답변입니다.

회신 확인과 감사

⟨V⟩ Thank you for contacting me.
연락 주신 것 감사합니다.

⟨V⟩ Thank you for your prompt reply.
당신의 빠른 답장 감사합니다.

⟨V⟩ This is to confirm receipt of your email dated April 15.
4월 15일자 당신의 이메일을 받았음을 확인하겠습니다.

답장 지연에 대한 사과

⟨V⟩ We sincerely apologize for the inconvenience.
불편을 드려 진심으로 사죄 드립니다.

⟨V⟩ I apologize for the delayed response. / I'm sorry for the late reply.
늦게 답장 드려 죄송합니다.

회신 요청

⟨V⟩ Would you follow up on this matter?
이 문제에 대해서 후속 조치를 해 주시겠습니까?

✅ We would appreciate a reply at your earliest convenience.
편하신 대로 최대한 빨리 답장해 주시면 감사하겠습니다.

✅ I look forward to hearing from you soon.
당신으로부터 곧 연락 받기를 기대합니다.

✅ Please reply to the following address.
답장은 아래의 주소로 보내 주세요.

✅ Please reply to all.
모두에게 답장하기로 해 주세요.

✅ Please respond to jjkim@tops.co.kr
답장은 jjkim@tops.co.kr로 해 주세요.

양해와 협조 요청

✅ I would appreciate your understanding.
이해해 주시면 고맙겠습니다.

✅ Your cooperation would be appreciated.
협조해 주시면 감사하겠습니다.

✅ Thank you in advance for your help.
도움에 대해 미리 감사 드리겠습니다.

✅ Thank you in advance for your kind consideration and cooperation.
당신의 친절한 배려와 협조 부탁 드립니다.

초대와 그에 대한 답변

✅ You are invited to a party.
당신을 파티에 초대합니다.

✅ Please let us know whether you can attend the party.
파티에 참석할 수 있는지 알려주시기 바랍니다.

Thank you for your kind invitation to your party.
당신의 파티에 초대해 주셔서 감사합니다.

I think I can make it.
참석할 수 있을 것 같습니다.

I'm afraid I can't make it.
죄송하지만 참석하지 못 할 것 같습니다.

약속 잡기, 변경하기

Please let me know when is convenient for you.
언제가 편하신지 알려 주세요.

Are you available this Saturday?
이번 주 토요일 괜찮으세요?

With regard to your scheduled visit to our office on March 5, I'm afraid that I have to ask you to change the date due to unexpected affairs.
3월 1일 예정된 우리 사무실 방문과 관련하여, 예상치 못한 일이 있어서 그러니 날짜를 좀 변경해 주셨으면 좋겠습니다.

Could we reschedule our appointment to an earlier time?
약속 시간을 좀 당길 수 있을까요?

I am writing to ask if we could postpone our appointment until next Monday?
우리 약속을 다음주 월요일로 미룰 수 있을지 여쭤 보려고 이메일 합니다.

첨부 화일 관련

I am attaching the file.
파일을 첨부합니다.

Please find the attached files.
첨부 파일을 보세요.

V Can you forward the attachment to me?

첨부된 것을 저에게 전달해 주시겠습니까?

V Attached is the document you asked.

첨부한 것은 당신이 요청하신 서류입니다.

V I forgot to attach the file in my previous mail, so I'm attaching it now.

이전 메일에서 파일 첨부하는 것을 잊어서 지금 첨부합니다.

V Please fill out the attached application.

첨부된 신청서를 작성해 주세요.

V I zipped the files.

파일들을 압축했습니다.

자료요청

V I am wondering if you can send us a booklet.

소책자를 하나 보내주실 수 있는지 궁금합니다.

V Could you fax the document to us, please?

문서를 팩스로 보내 주실 수 있나요?

요청받은 자료 보내기

V This is the information you requested.

요청하신 자료를 보냅니다.

메일 수신에 문제가 있는 경우

V I sent you an e-mail but it bounced back.

이메일을 보냈는데 되돌아왔어요.

V Your mail box exceeded its quota.

당신의 메일 박스는 용량이 초과되었습니다.

Business English for Secretaries

부재시 수신 이메일 처리

☑ This is an automatic reply.

I'm on a business trip until September 10th.

Please refer any urgent matters to my secretary, Amanda Clifford.

이것은 자동 회신입니다. / 저는 9월 10일까지 출장입니다.
급한 용무는 제 비서 Amanda Clifford에게 문의 하세요.

☑ I'll be away from my e-mail during the period.

저는 그 기간 동안 메일을 확인할 수 없습니다.

☑ I'll be in touch with you as soon as possible when I return.

돌아오는 대로 빨리 연락 드리겠습니다.

맺음말 쓰기

☑ Let's keep in touch.

계속 연락합시다.

☑ Please do not hesitate to contact me any time.

언제든지 연락해 주십시오.

☑ Please feel free to contact us.

망설이지 말고 저희에게 연락 주세요.

☑ Take care.

안녕. (윗 사람에게는 쓰지 않는다.)

☑ Give my best regards to Sally.

Sally 에게 안부 전해 주세요.

축하, 위로

☑ Congratulations on your promotion!

승진을 축하합니다.

☑ I am so sorry to hear that.

참 안됐습니다.

Sample E-mail   1

To: "Claire Morris" clairem@business.com
Cc: All Staff
From: "Alex Howard" alexh@business.com
Subject: Welcome to Business Co!

Dear Morris,

Welcome to our company!

It's a pleasure to welcome you to the staff of Business Co. We are excited to have you join our company, and we hope you will enjoy working at our company.

On the first Monday of each month we hold a special staff lunch to welcome any new employees. Please be sure to come next week to meet all of our senior staff and any other new staff members who have joined us in April. JoAnn Kim will e-mail you with further details.

If you have any questions, please do not hesitate to contact me. You can reach me at my e-mail address or on my office line at 267 9828.

Regards,

Alex Howard, HR Manager
Business Co.
Phone: (456) 267 9828 Fax: (456) 267 9825

alexh@business.com

To: "eunymay" eunymay@personal.com
From: "Risa Smith"   risa@costumes.com
Subject: An Exciting Feature from Costumes Co.

Dear Ms. May,

As a Costumes Co. client, we invite you to create your online account! Your account contains all of your client information which you can update as needed in our safe and secure online environment.

Additionally, you will have access to the following programs specifically designed for clients:

- **Refer a Friend**: receive one year free annual storage if you refer a friend.
- **Special Repeat Client Pricing**: Costumes Co. offers a discount to returning clients.
- **Newsroom:** get the latest news about costumes.

As always, we value and appreciate your feedback. Please contact clientcare@costumes.com with any questions and comments you may have.

Warm regards,

Risa Smith
Client Care, Costumes Co.
132 Pinetree St. | Dallas, TX 13523
Phone : (214) 365 7453 Fax : (214) 365 7458
risa@costumes.com

To: "ryanlee" ryanlee@personal.com

From: "Gabriella Rothon" gabriellarothon@eshopping.com

Subject: Regarding Our Meeting for this Monday

Dear Mr. Lee:

I am writing to you concerning the meeting arranged for this Monday. I am afraid something urgent has come up and I will not be able to attend. Can we postpone the meeting until next week? I can make it any time Tuesday or Wednesday.

I apologize for any inconvenience this may cause, and I look forward to hearing from you.

Sincerely,

Gabriella Rothon

Accounting Manager

E-shopping Company

Tel : (534) 645 5764

gabriellarothon@eshopping.com

팩스(Fax)는 Facsimile의 약어이며 간단한 서류를 보내기에 적합하다. 단, 보안상의 문제로 기밀 서류(confidential document)는 Fax로 보내지 않는다.

팩스로 서류를 보낼 때는 팩스 표지 (Fax cover)를 만들어 보낸다. 회사에서 사용하고 있는 것이 없는 경우 간단하게 만들어 쓸 수 있어야 한다. 팩스 표지에 간단한 메시지를 써서 보낼 수도 있다.

팩스에는 체계적인 수신, 송신을 위해서 참조 번호(reference number)들을 기입하는 경우도 있다.

팩스를 보낼 때는 표지에 페이지 수를 잘 기입하도록 한다. 장문의 서류를 보내거나 받을 때는 페이지 수를 잘 확인하여 빠진 것이 없는지 확인해야 한다.

 참고

팩스 수신의 문제

- 팩스를 다 수신하지 못 했을 경우

  Sorry but couldn't receive complete fax. Page 24 and 26 are missing. Please try again.

- 팩스가 흐릿하여 잘 안 보이는 경우

  The fax message is not clear. Will you send it us again?

Sample Fax 1

Date	Aug. 12, 2014	Number of Pages : 1 (including this)	
Sender	Jeffrey Duncan	Recipient	Kevin Meier
	Business Daily		ESHN Advertising Co.
	Fax : +82 2 534 6453		Fax : + 1 324 534 3314
	Tel : +82 2 534 6457		Tel : + 1 324 534 7564

MESSAGE:

Thank you for your fax of Aug. 10 requesting a meeting on the marketing plan. However, I regret that I have another appointment at that time and am unavailable to attend the meeting.

I appreciate your understanding.

Jeffrey

Jeffrey Duncan

Editor

Advantage Supplies Inc.

243 Wellington St.
Ann Arbor, MI 48104
TEL. 734 267 1728
FAX. 734 267 8472

Debby Weston
Purchasing Manager
PRAM International Inc.
Fax: (324) 371–1120

Nov. 22, 2013

Re: Your fax #023 dated Nov. 21, 2013

Dear Ms. Weston:

Thank you for your fax. Most of all, we apologize for the delay in shipping your order.

We normally keep to our delivery dates, but in this case our supplies shipped to us late. Your order will be shipped today, and the date of delivery will be November 27.

We are very sorry for the inconvenience that may have been caused, and will make every effort to prevent a recurrence.

Sincerely yours,

Anna Sullivan

Anna Sullivan
Customer Service
Advantage Supplies

Fax Cover Sheet

To:	From:
Fax:	Date:
Phone:	Pages:
Re:	CC:

☐ Urgent ☐ For Review ☐ Please Comment ☐ Please Reply ☐ Please Recycle

Comments:

메모는 보통 회사 내에서 동료들끼리 보내는 메시지로 회사의 여러 가지 행사나 정책, 교육 기회 안내 등을 그 내용으로 한다. 사무 서신에 비해서 형식이 자유롭고 보내는 사람의 이름도 이니셜로 표기되는 경우도 많으며 친근한 표현들이 많이 쓰인다. 최근에는 이메일의 형태로 보내지거나 회사 사내 사이트의 게시판(Bulletin Board)에 올려지는 경우가 많다.

Sample Memo 1

Memorandum

From: JSL
To: Department Heads
Date: July 5, 2014
Subject: In-house Accounting Class

1. From July 21, Monday, Accounting class will be held in the library. There will be two sessions: intermediate level (11 a.m.) and advanced level (2 p.m.). Please encourage your staff to attend one of the sessions.

2. Please send me the names of all interested staff by July 12. They will be given a test so that we can decide which of the classes is best for them.

Memorandum

To :   Employees of Boston Holdings

From :   John R. Taylor, Head of General Affairs Department

Date: 15 February 2015

Subject :   Security System

Please be aware that the security system for this building is going to be replaced as of January 1 next year. According to our new policy, all employees must carry their photo ID cards. Starting January 1 of the next year, anyone without proper identification will not be allowed into the premises.

In the case that you don't yet have your photo ID card, submit the following items to the General Affairs Department by December 20.

  1) Passport-size photograph

  2) A copy of social security card

  3) Signed copy of your employment contract

Thank you for your cooperation.

JRT

출장 일정표(itinerary) 작성요령

출장 기간 전체의 일정이 한눈에 들어오도록 작성하고, 상사가 휴대하기 편한 크기로 한 부 더 준비하는 것이 좋다.

일정표에 들어가야 하는 사항

❶ 출발/귀국 일시, 교통편 – 시간, 공항, 비행기 편명, 연결편, 소요시간, 기차역 이름 등을 정확하게 기재하되 현지시각(local time)으로 한다.

❷ 숙박장소 및 연락처 – 호텔 이름 및 주소, 전화번호까지 적어두어 출장 가는 사람의 편의를 고려한다.

❸ 방문처, 면담자 – 방문 장소의 주소와 전화번호도 적어두며, 만날 사람의 이름과 직위도 기재한다.

❹ 방문 목적을 정확히 기재한다.

❺ 식사장소 및 인원– 주최자 및 참석자, 식사 장소를 정확히 기재한다.

Sample Business Itinerary   1

ITINERARY FOR THE VISIT OF MR. KIM
TO THE C&C FACTORY

23 JANUARY

9:00	Arrival
9:05 - 9:45	Meeting with the Overseas Sales Manager (Conference Room 215)
9:45 - 10:15	Company Presentation Video
!0:15 - 11:00	Demonstration of the Online System
11:00 - 12:00	Meeting with Professional Engineers
12:00 - 2:00	Lunch with Overseas Sales Manager and Marketing Director (Restaurant La Seine)
2:30 - 3:30	Tour of C&C Factory
3:30 - 4:10	Final Discussion with the Overseas Sales Manager
5:00	Car to Terminal 7, Seattle Airport
6:30	Flight to Texas, DT107

Itinerary for Mr. David Stevenson

\<From Jan. 6 to 8, 2015 in Seoul, Korea>

One-on-One Meetings, Luncheon Seminar & Dinner

Time	Details	Attendee(s) + Car Arrangements
Jan. 6 (Sun)		
4:25 PM	KE 082 JFK 12:00 (-1) to ICN 16:25	Mr. Kim / M: +82 10 8372 1888 / Car Plate: #4837
	Move to The Westin Hotel	**Pls meet the driver holding name board at the gate*
Jan. 7 (Mon)		
9:30 AM	*Move to Hankook Bank*	Mr. Kim / M: +82 10 8372 1888 / Car Plate: #4837
	Pick-up at The Westin Hotel	**Pls meet Jason Lee at the hotel lobby*
10:00 AM	**Hankook Bank** 139, Namdaemun-ro, Jung-gu, Seoul	**Kuhyun Jung**, MD / Management Dept. **DIC: Jason Lee will join* Mr. Kim / M: +82 10 8372 1888 / Car Plate: #4837
12:00 PM	*Move to The Hilton Hotel*	Mr. Kim / M: +82 10 8372 1888 / Car Plate: #4837
12:30 PM	**Luncheon Seminar**	Clients arranged by DIC Korea Market Sales Team
	3F, Orchid Hall The Hilton Hotel	
2:30 PM	Move to DIC	Mr. Park / M: +82 10 6352 3748 / Car Plate: #8574
3:00 PM	**Daehan Investment Corporation** 25, Yaksu-2-ro, Jung-gu, Seoul	**Junho Kim**, CEO **Helen Lee**, Head of Equity **Mark Whang**, Head of Fixed Income

4:30 PM	*Move to The Westin Hotel*	Mr. Park / M: +82 10 6352 3748 / Car Plate: #8574
7:00 PM	**Dinner**	
	2F, Rose Hall The Westin Hotel	**Helen Lee**, Head of Equity **Mark Whang**, Head of Fixed Income
Jan. 8 (Tue)		
7:20 AM	*Move to Incheon Airport*	Mr. Park / M: +82 10 6352 3748 / Car Plate: #8574
	KE 082 ICN 10:05 to JFK 11:20	

Contact Point

DIC	Office	Mobile
Junho Kim	+82 2 5837 2777	+82 10 2847 2843
Helen Lee	+82 2 5837 2748	+82 10 2948 0091
Mark Whang	+82 2 5837 2829	+82 10 1980 2882
Jason Lee	+82 2 5837 2739	+82 10 5887 3882
Assistant	**Office**	**Mobile**
Kay Lee	+82 2 5837 2857	+82 10 5792 2441
		+82 10 9377 5764
Driver	**Car Plate Number**	**Mobile**
Mr. Kim	#4837	+82 10 8372 1888
Mr. Park	#8574	+82 10 6352 3748

BUSINESS ENGLiISH for SECRETARIES

Presentation

Presentation

프리젠테이션을 위한 기본적 표현을 익히고 시각 자료를 영어로 설명하는
연습을 한다.

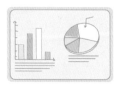

Presentation Basics

영어 프리젠테이션(presentation)을 할 때는 크게 세 부분으로 나누어 하는 것이 좋다.

서론에서 프리젠테이션의 목적과 말하고자 하는 주제를 소개한다. 또 발표 시간이 얼마나 소요되는지, 질의 응답은 어떻게 할지를 미리 밝히는 것이 좋다.

본론에서는 주제와 관련하여 객관적이면서도 설득력 있는 주장을 하되, 신빙성 있는 자료와 근거를 밝혀야 한다. 효과적 자료와 근거를 제시하기 위해 시각자료(visual aids)를 적절히 사용하는 것이 중요하다. 특히 파워포인트(Powerpoint)를 이용한 발표가 많으므로, 이를 효과적으로 제작하고 읽으면서 진행해 나가는 기술이 필요하다.

결론에서는 이제까지 말한 내용을 요약, 확인하면서 발표를 마무리하면 된다. 마지막으로 질문을 받고 답하는 시간을 갖는다.

영어 프리젠테이션에서 발표자가 주의할 점은 빨리 말하려 하기보다는 적절한 속도로 또박또박 말해야 한다는 것이다. 그리고 중요한 대목에서는 잠시 말을 끊고 쉬어가며 하는 것이 좋다.

Business English for Secretaries

Key Expressions for Presentation

1 사회자의 발표 전 전달사항 및 장내 정리

☑ Please turn off your cell phones or put them on silent mode.
핸드폰을 끄거나 소리가 울리지 않게 해주세요.

☑ Please put your cell phones on vibrate.
핸드폰을 진동으로 해 주세요.

☑ Today's presentation will be proceeding as follows.
First(ly)···.. Second(ly)···.. Third(ly)······.. Finally.
오늘 발표는 다음과 같이 진행될 것입니다.
첫째, ～. 둘째, ～. 셋째, ～. 마지막으로 ～

☑ Presentations will be given by Cyndy Jung, Jane Smith, and John Kim.
Cyndy Jung, Jane Smith, John Kim이 발표를 하겠습니다.

☑ Each presentation will have approximately 10 minutes.
발표에는 약 10분씩 시간이 주어집니다.

☑ 10 minutes of question time is allocated for each presentation.
각 프리젠테이션에 대해 10분의 질문 시간이 주어집니다.

☑ There will be a short discussion after each presentation.
각 프리젠테이션 다음에는 짧은 토론이 있겠습니다.

☑ Please complete the questionnaire in front of you after all presentations.
모든 프리젠테이션이 끝난 뒤에는 앞에 있는 설문지에 답해주세요.

☑ A buffet lunch will be provided after the presentation in the next room.
프리젠테이션이 끝나면 옆 방에서 점심으로 뷔페가 제공됩니다.

② 사회자(presider)의 발표자(presenter) 소개

Ⅴ May I have your attention please?
주목해 주시겠습니까?

Ⅴ Let me introduce today's presenters to you one by one.
오늘 발표자를 한 사람씩 소개하겠습니다.

Ⅴ From your left, Cyndy Jung, Jane Smith, and John Kim.
왼쪽에서부터 Cyndy Jung, Jane Smith, John Kim 입니다.

Ⅴ Now, I'd like to introduce the presenters to you.
이제, 발표자를 소개하겠습니다.

Ⅴ The next presenter is Jane Smith.
다음 발표자는 Jane Smith 입니다.

③ 발표자 서두 인사

Ⅴ Thank you for giving me a chance to speak to you.
발표할 기회를 주셔서 감사합니다.

Ⅴ I am pleased to extend my warmest greetings to all of you.
여러분 모두를 진심으로 환영합니다.

Ⅴ I'd like to welcome you to the presentation today.
오늘 프리젠테이션에 오신 것을 환영합니다.

④ 발표자 자기소개 및 발표 준비

Ⅴ I'm Cyndy Jung of Planning Team.
저는 기획팀의 Cyndy Jung 입니다.

Ⅴ I'm Jane Smith and I'm responsible for finance at B&G.
저는 Jane Smith 이며, B&G의 재정을 담당하고 있습니다.

☑ Let me start my presentation.

프리젠테이션을 시작하겠습니다.

☑ Please interrupt me at any time if you have any questions.

질문이 있으시면 언제라도 질문해 주세요.

☑ I'll take questions at the end of my presentation.

프리젠테이션이 끝나고 질문 받겠습니다.

5 주제 소개 / presentation의 목적

The subject of this presentation is ~

My objective is ~

I will talk about ~

I would like to emphasize ~

This presentation is designed to ~

The purpose of today's presentation is~

☑ The subject of this presentation is newly revised Early Retirement Plan.

이번 프리젠테이션의 주제는 새로 개정된 조기 퇴직 계획입니다.

☑ My objective is to give you an overview of new operating system.

저의 목적은 새로운 운영체계에 대한 개요를 보여주기 위한 것 입니다.

☑ I will talk about some tips for creating attractive websites.

저는 멋진 웹사이트를 만드는 몇 가지 비법을 알려드리고자 합니다.

☑ I would like to emphasize the profits from investment in public sector.

저는 공공부문 투자의 이익에 대해 강조하고자 합니다.

☑ This presentation is designed to give you information about our new product.

이 프리젠테이션은 여러분에게 저희 신상품에 대한 정보를 주는 데 목적을 둡니다.

☑ The purpose of today's presentation is to discuss follow-up measures.

오늘 발표의 목적은 후속 조치를 논의하기 위한 것입니다.

6 Presentation 본론 진행

Now let me begin by ~

이제 ~로 시작 하겠습니다.

OK. Let's start with ~

자 ~로 시작 합시다.

Let's take a look at page 15 of your handout.

Handout 15 페이지를 봅시다.

Would you please take a look at this table?

이 표를 보시겠습니까?

According to a recently published survey, ~

최근 발표된 조사에 따르면,

I'd like to make it clear that~

~을 분명히 하고 싶습니다.

This is illustrated in Figure 11(a).

이것은 그림11(a)에 설명되어 있습니다.

For your reference, let me explain ~

참고로, ~을 설명 드리겠습니다.

If you have a look at this first graph, ~

이 첫 번째 ~그래프를 보시면~

As you can see from the bar graph, ~

막대 그래프에서 보듯이,

I'd like to illustrate this point with some examples.

이점에 대해서 몇 가지 예를 들어 설명하겠습니다.

Let's move on to the next slide.

다음 슬라이드로 넘어갑시다.

Let me skip item 1 and move on to the item 2.

1번 항목은 건너뛰고 바로 2번 항목으로 넘어가겠습니다.

So far, I've talked about ~

지금까지 ~에 대하여 말씀 드렸습니다.

- Now let me begin by asking a question.

  자 이제 질문을 하면서 시작해 보겠습니다.

- OK. Let's start with the statistics.

  자, 통계자료로 시작하겠습니다.

- According to a recently published survey, our market share increased by 15%.

  최근 발표된 조사에 따르면, 우리 시장 점유율이 15% 증가하였습니다.

- I'd like to make it clear that labor productivity growth is due to technical cooperation with C&C Industries.

  노동 생산성 향상은 C&C 산업과 기술제휴 덕분임을 분명히 하고 싶습니다.

- For your reference, let me explain China's retail price index.

  참고로, 중국의 소매물가 지수를 말씀 드리겠습니다.

- If you have a look at this first graph, you will notice the percentage of the population using the Internet.

  첫 번째 그래프를 보시면, 인터넷을 사용하는 인구 비율을 알 수 있을 것입니다.

- As you can see from the bar graph, we have increased our market share in South Asia for years.

  막대 그래프에서 보듯이, 우리는 수년간 남아시아 시장 점유율을 높여왔습니다.

- So far, I've talked about expected gains from mergers. Now I'll talk about expected losses from mergers.

  지금까지 합병의 예상되는 잇점에 대해 말했습니다. 이제 합병으로 인해 예상되는 손해에 대해 말씀 드리겠습니다.

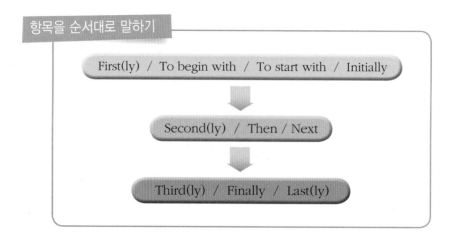

항목을 순서대로 말하기

First(ly) / To begin with / To start with / Initially

Second(ly) / Then / Next

Third(ly) / Finally / Last(ly)

7 Presentation 마무리하기

Ⓥ That brings me to the end of my presentation.

이렇게 해서 제 프리젠테이션을 마칠 시간이 되었습니다.

Ⓥ OK, that ends my talk.

자 이제 마치도록 하겠습니다.

Ⓥ That covers all I wanted to say today.

이로써 오늘 제가 하고자 했던 말은 다하였습니다.

Ⓥ I would like to close this presentation by summarizing what I have just said.

지금까지 말씀드린 것을 요약하면서 이번 발표를 마치고자 합니다..

Ⓥ Let me just run over the key points again.

다시 중요 사항을 짚어보겠습니다.

Ⓥ Before I finish, let me just go over these points.

마치기 전에 이 점들을 검토해 보겠습니다.

Ⓥ You can find more detailed information on the booklet I handed out to you.

제가 드린 소책자에서 더 상세한 자료를 보실 수 있습니다

Ⓥ If you have any questions, please go ahead. I'll be happy to answer them for you.

질문 있으시면 해주세요. 기꺼이 답하겠습니다..

Ⓥ I will now take any questions you may have.

이제 질문을 받도록 하겠습니다.

Ⓥ Do you have any comments or questions?

의견이나 질문 있으십니까?

Ⓥ I would be happy to answer any of your questions.

이제 어떤 질문이든 하시면 기꺼이 답하겠습니다.

Ⓥ Now I'd like to invite your comments.

이제 여러분의 의견을 받겠습니다.

☑ Is that OK? / Is that clear now?

(질문에 답을 한 후) 충분한 설명이 되었습니까? 이제 분명해 졌습니까?

☑ Can we move on?

(질문에 답하고 나서) 넘어가도 되겠습니까?

☑ Thank for your attention.

주목해 주셔서 감사 합니다

☑ Thank you for listening.

경청해 주셔서 감사합니다.

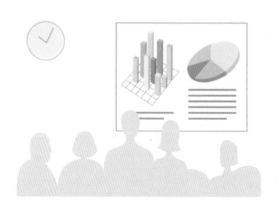

2 Visual Aids

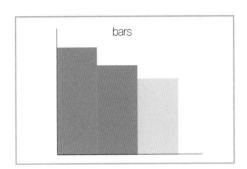

(Vertical) Bar Graph

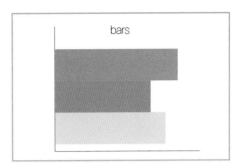

(Horizontal) Bar Graph

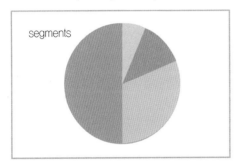

Pie Graph

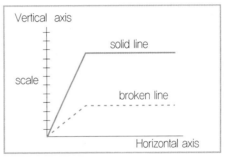

Broken Line Graph

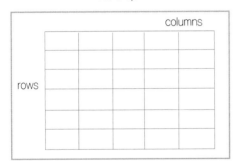

Table

Figure

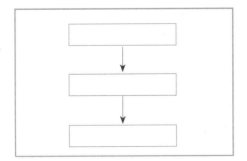

Flow Chart

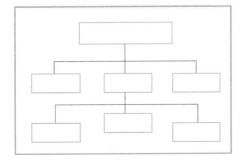

Organigram

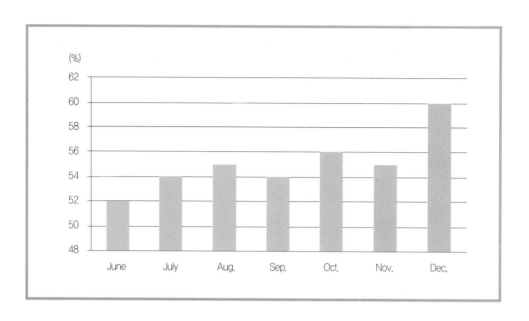

There was no observable change in the rate of employment from June to November.
고용률에 있어서 6월부터 11월까지 주목할 만한 변화는 없었습니다.

But the rate of employment has peaked at 60% in December.
그러나 12월에는 고용률이 60%로 최고치를 기록했습니다.

This figure is five percent higher than a month ago.
이 수치는 한 달 전 보다 5퍼센트 높은 것입니다.

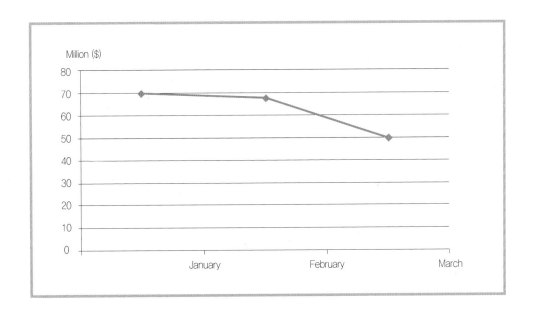

Our turnover has decreased slightly in February.

2월에는 우리 거래액이 약간 감소하였습니다.

But it has decreased by almost 20 million dollars in March.

그러나 3월에는 거의 2천만 달러나 줄었습니다.

The fluctuation range was big between February and March.

2월과 3월 사이의 변동 폭이 컸습니다.

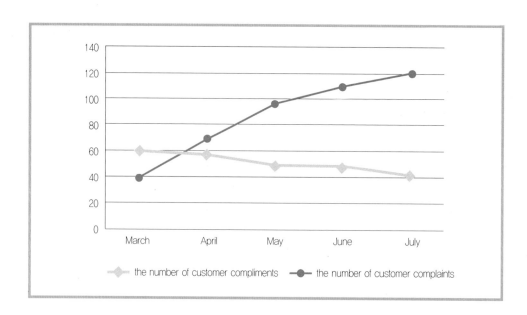

the number of customer compliments　　the number of customer complaints

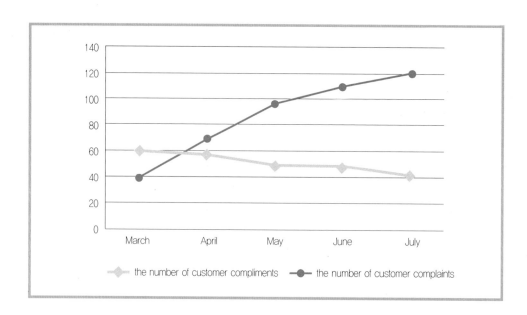

☑ According to the graph above, the number of customer complaints has sharply increased while that of customer compliments has gradually decreased since March.
위의 그래프에 따르면, 3월 이후로 고객 칭찬 건수는 서서히 줄어드는 반면 고객 불만 건수는 급격히 증가하였다.

☑ The number of customer complaints has tripled to 120 over the past four months.
지난 4개월간 고객 불만 건수는 세 배로 증가해서 120건이 되었다.

☑ As of July, the number of customer complaints is about triple that of customer compliments.
7월부로 고객 불만건수는 칭찬 건수의 약 3배이다.

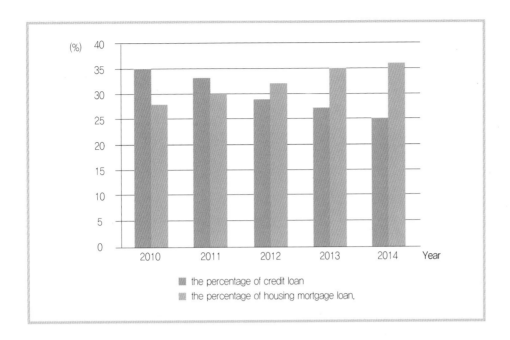

✔ According to the graph, in 2010 the percentage of credit loan exceeded that of housing mortgage loan.

그래프에 따르면, 2010년 신용대출 비율이 주택담보대출을 넘어섰습니다.

✔ From 2010 to 2014, however, the percentage of credit loan decreased from 35% to 25%.

그러나 2010년부터 2014년까지 신용대출의 비율이 35%에서 25%로 줄어들었습니다.

✔ In the same period, the rate of housing mortgage loan showed a constant increase.

같은 기간, 주택담보대출의 비율은 지속적인 증가를 보여줬습니다.

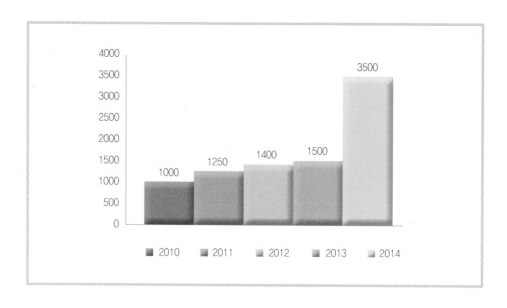

🏆 The vertical axis represents the number of cars sold and the horizontal axis shows the period of time.

세로축은 판매된 차의 수를 나타내고, 가로축은 기간을 나타냅니다.

🏆 This graph clearly shows that the sales have more than doubled since 2013.

이 그래프는 2013년 이래로 판매가 두 배 이상이 되었음을 분명히 보여줍니다.

🏆 It shows that the sales have reached the peak in 2014.

판매량이 2014년에 최고치를 기록했다는 것을 보여줍니다.

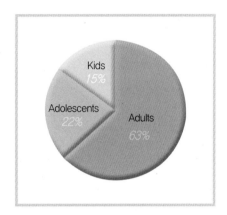

The pie graph (pie chart) above illustrates that adults over the age of 20 account for 63 percent of the total sunscreen users.

위의 원 그래프는 20세 이상 성인이 전체 썬스크린 사용자의 63%를 차지함을 보여줍니다.

Adolescents aged 13 to 19 are the second largest sunscreen users, but they are a little over one third of adult sunscreen users.

13세에서 19세 청소년이 두 번째로 큰 썬스크린 사용자이지만 성인 썬스크린 사용자의 3분의 1 을 조금 넘습니다.

Kids under the age of 12 account for only 15 percent, and they are slightly less than one fourth of adult sunscreen users.

12세 이하 아이들은 겨우 15 퍼센트 차지하는데, 성인 썬스크린 사용자의 4분의 1보다 조금 적습니다

1 Reading Pictogram

June	🌂 🌂 🌂 🌂 🌂 🌂 🌂 🌂 🌂 🌂 🌂 🌂 🌂 🌂
July	🌂 🌂 🌂 🌂 🌂 🌂 🌂 🌂
August	🌂 🌂 🌂 🌂 🌂

| 🌂 | = | one day of rain |

▼ This pictogram has been drawn to represent days of rain during the summer months.
이 그림 그래프(pictogram)는 여름 동안 비 온 날을 보여주기 위해 그려졌습니다.

▼ In the pictogram, each umbrella represents one day of rain.
그림 그래프(pictogram)에서 우산 하나는 비 온 날 입니다.

▼ 14 days of rain were recorded in June.
6월에는 비가 온 날이 14일인 것으로 기록되어 있습니다.

Month	Average Daytime Temperature (℃)	Average Nighttime Temperature (℃)
January	-1	-7
February	3	-1
March	11	0
April	17	5
May	21	12
June	25	20
July	32	27
August	30	25
September	25	12
October	17	5
November	11	3
December	0	-5

Row ➡

Column ⬇

	Column1	Column 2	Column 3	Column 4
Row1	Row1 Column1	Row1 Column2	Row1 Column3	Row1 Column4
Row2	Row2 Column1	Row2 Column2	Row2 Column3	Row2 Column4

✓ The second column represents average daytime temperature and the third column represents average nighttime temperature.
두 번째 열은 평균 낮 기온을 나타내고, 세 번째 열은 평균 밤 기온을 나타냅니다.

✓ Reading down the column, you will see that the highest average daytime temperature is 32℃ in July.
세로줄을 읽어 내려오면, 가장 높은 평균 낮 기온은 7월의 32℃ 라는 것을 알게 될 것입니다.

✓ Take a look at the fourth row from the bottom. We can see the greatest daily temperature range occuring during September.
아래에서 네 번째 행을 보세요. 9월에 가장 큰 일교차가 나타남을 볼 수 있습니다.

시각 자료 읽기에 필요한 표현

Bolded Underlined Italicized	Word(s) Phrase(s) Sentence(s)	
The (light blue) shaded The unshaded The hatched The (red) colored	Section Area	Indicate(s) Represent(s) Show(s)
The vertical axis The horizontal axis The solid line The broken line The dotted line The curved line		

Vocabulary

- ≫ Bolded   굵은 활자체로된
- ≫ Underlined   밑줄친
- ≫ Italicized   이탤릭체로된
- ≫ (light blue) shaded   (밝은 파란색으로) 음영처리된
- ≫ unshaded   음영처리되지 않은
- ≫ hatched   빗금친
- ≫ (red) colored   (빨간색으로) 색칠된
- ≫ vertical axis   세로축
- ≫ horizontal axis   가로축
- ≫ solid line   직선
- ≫ broken line   절선, 파선
- ≫ dotted line   점선
- ≫ curved line   곡선
- ≫ indicate / represent / show   나타내다. 보여주다

3 Discussion

다른 사람의 의견을 물어 볼 때

- What do you think about this?
- Scott, what are your views on this?
- Do you have any other thoughts?

다른 사람에게 자기의 말을 이해하고 있는지 확인할 때

- Do you see what I mean?
- Are you with me?
- Does that seem to make sense?
- So is that clear?

상대방이 말한 것을 이해 못 할 때

- Sorry, could you say that again, please?
- Sorry, I didn't quite understand.
- Sorry, I'm not quite with you.
- I'm sorry, I didn't quite follow you there.
- I'm sorry, I didn't catch what you said.
- What is your point?

다른 사람이 말하는 중에 끼어들어서 의견을 말하고 싶을 때

- Sorry to interrupt, but I'd just like to say that…
- If I could make a point here…
- Could I make a suggestion?

상대방의 말에 동의할 때

- Ⓥ I agree with that suggestion, because…
- Ⓥ That's just what I was thinking.
- Ⓥ That's a good point.
- Ⓥ I couldn't agree more.

상대방의 말에 동의하지 않을 때

- Ⓥ I don't quite agree with that point because…
- Ⓥ I see what you mean, but…
- Ⓥ That's true, but on the other hand…
- Ⓥ I can't agree with you on that point.
- Ⓥ I see things differently.

자신의 의견 말하기

- Ⓥ In my opinion,
- Ⓥ If you ask me,

주장을 말하기

- Ⓥ I'm sure that~
- Ⓥ You can argue that~, but~

논점을 지적하면서 말하기

- Ⓥ As far as ~ is concerned,
- Ⓥ With regard to~

거론할 내용을 도입하기

- ☑ Normally,
- ☑ Generally speaking,

근거를 제시하기

- ☑ In light of~
- ☑ Judging from~

화제 바꾸기

- ☑ By the way,

오해를 바로잡기

- ☑ That's not what I meant.
- ☑ You have misunderstood my point.
- ☑ You are missing my point.

재고할 것을 제의

- ☑ I think we need more time to consider this.
- ☑ Could you please think it over?

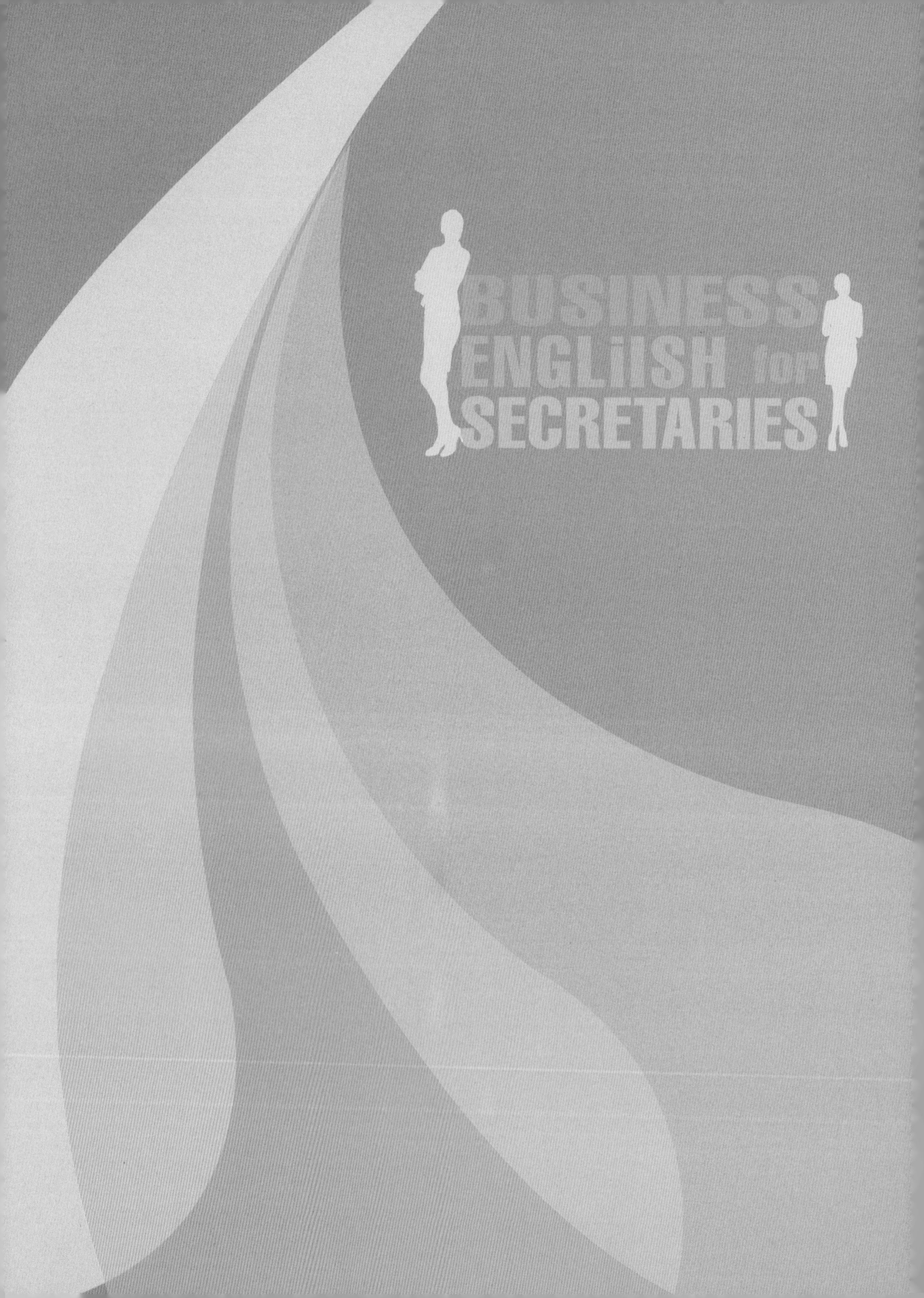
BUSINESS
ENGLiSH for
SECRETARIES

Resume / Cover Letter

Unit

7

Resume / Cover Letter

영어 이력서, Cover letter 작성법을 익히고, 자기소개서, 면접에 필요한 기본
표현을 연습하여 비서직 취업에 대비한다.

1 Resume

영문 이력서는 resume 또는 CV (curriculum vitae: 라틴어로 "life story" 를 의미) 라고 한다. 이력서에는 학력, 경력, 성취한 바, 수상 내역, 특기 사항 등을 쓴다.

이력서 쓸 때 유의할 점

❶ 이력서를 종이로 인쇄할 때는 흰색 또는 미색의 고급 규격 종이에 인쇄하도록 한다.

❷ 이름과 주소, 연락처는 상단 중앙에 두고 이름은 두꺼운 글자체로 강조한다.

❸ 한 장을 넘지 않게 쓴다.

❹ 이력서 내용 중 중요한 부분인 학교 이름이나 근무한 회사 이름 등은 두꺼운 글자체나 이탤릭체 혹은 밑줄 등으로 강조한다.

❺ 보통 학력이나 경력은 역연대기순으로(최근의 것이 앞으로 나오게) 쓴다.

❻ 지원하고자 하는 직업에 관계되는 정보나 경험 등을 포함시킨다.

❼ 이력서는 몇 번에 걸쳐 교정(proofreading)을 보아야 한다. 절대 오타가 있어서는 안되므로 되도록이면 다른 사람에게도 교정을 부탁한다.

❽ 인쇄된 이력서를 제출할 때는 커버레터(cover letter)도 동봉한다.

❾ 글자체나 글씨 크기는 인쇄된 이력서의 모양에 따라 보기 좋게 한다. 대개 Arial 글자체로 하며 글자 크기는 Arial의 경우 10 (내용이 많을 경우) 또는 11 (내용이 적을 경우)로 한다.

YOUR NAME

ADDRESS

PHONE (010) 000-0000 • E-MAIL KIM@BUSINESS.COM

OBJECTIVE

EDUCATION

20xx - 20xx School/Organization Name City, Province
Diploma/Certificate/Major
Details of education completed

20xx - 20xx School/Organization Name City, Province
Diploma/Certificate/Major
Details of education completed

WORK EXPERIENCE

20xx - 20xx Company/Organization Name City, Province
Job Title
Details of position

20xx - 20xx Company/Organization Name City, Province
Job Title
Details of position

SKILLS

REFERENCES

References and letters of recommendation available on request

Sample Resume   1

DONG IL KIM

13 Banpo-ro, Seocho-gu | Seoul | 010 9482 8427 | dongilkim02@iolinemail.co.kr

OBJECTIVE

An entry-level administrative or management position with a small or medium sized business

EDUCATION

Bachelor of Science, Secretarial Administration   Expected 2016 Feb.

Hankuk University, Kyunggi

- Major: Secretarial Administration
- Minor: Business Administration
- Related course works: Accountings, business laws, economics, computer programming, management

SKILLS & ABILITIES

Management in Student Association of Hankook University

- Organized and implemented school promotion event which invited approximately 300 local high school students
- Coordinated and organized annual festival event for two years
- Developed and implemented new fundraising program

Academics
- GPA: 4.1/4.3
- Honor Student Scholarship for two years

Language & Computer Skills
- Fluent in English (TOEIC score: 820)
- Good command of Chinese
- Proficient at Microsoft Office

EXPERIENCE

Assistant Manager   2013 Mar. to 2015 Feb.

Hankuk University, Kyunggi

- Hankuk University General Students Association
- Responsible for promotions and advertisement of Students Association

Server   2014 Mar. to 2016 Feb.

café Today

- Provided excellent table service and learned a lot regarding customer satisfaction in a cafe

Seo Hyun Kim

#102-374, Hue Apt. Shinsa-dong, Kangnam-gu
Seoul, Korea
010 3764 9183
seohyun@hanjin.ac.kr

OBJECTIVE

To obtain a secretarial position

EDUCATION

Hanjin University, Seoul, KOREA
B.A. in Business Administration

2010-2014

Studied Economics, Marketing, Accounting, Customer Relations etc.
Minor: English Language & Literature
Overall GPA: 3.9 / 4.3

RELATED EXPERIENCE

LMC Marketing Co, Incheon, Kyunggi
Secretary
- Organized the filing system for a branch office, performed general office work and assisted bank businesses

- Assisted in the creation of an agency-wide database

- Made various documents utilizing MS OFFICE

2014-2015

Hanjin University, Seoul, Korea

Receptionist
- Processed and filed incoming student applications and sent brochures to prospective students

Summer 2012

- Assisted in the organization of the Department's computer classes and performed general office work

LANGUAGES

- Written and oral fluency in English
- Conversational proficiency in Japanese

Business English for Secretaries

2 Cover Letter

커버레터(Cover Letter) 쓸 때 유의점

커버레터(Cover letter)는 이력서 보낼 때 같이 보내는 간단한 양식의 자기 소개서이다. 커버레터(Cover letter)에 들어가야 할 내용은 다음과 같다.

1. 그 직업에 지원을 희망함
2. 직업에 대한 정보를 ~에서 얻었음
3. 자신이 그 직업에 적합하다고 생각하는 이유
4. 필요시 더 많은 자료를 보낼 수 있음
5. 인터뷰를 희망함
6. 자신의 연락처

위 내용을 정중하고 간략하게 쓰도록 한다. 커버 레터에는 자신의 출생, 성장, 가족 관계나 모든 학력, 꼭 필요하지 않은 경력 등을 장황하게 쓰지 않는 것이 좋다.

영문 사무 서신의 양식에 잘 맞추어야 함은 기본이다. 지원자를 평가할 때 이력서상에 드러난 내용 뿐 아니라 이력서와 커버 레터를 양식에 맞게 쓰는 능력 자체가 평가 기준이 됨을 명심한다.

Sumi Park
#102-504 Rainbow Apt.
Bokwang-dong, Yongsan-gu
Seoul, Korea

May 12th, 2013

Personnel Dept.
Haeil Industries
1-35 Guro-dong, Guro-gu
Seoul, Korea

To whom it may concern:

I'm writing to apply for the position of secretary as advertised in the May edition of *Business Monthly*.

I am a fully-trained secretary with a diploma in Secretarial Administration and I have 6-month internship experience. I currently study at Hankook University in Seoul, Korea.

I would like to apply for the position advertised as I feel I am qualified for the job. I have experience working at a law firm as a secretary. I have excellent computer skills and good command of English. I am sociable and well organized, and I enjoy working with people.

I enclose a copy of my CV and a completed application form. I look forward to hearing from you soon.

Sincerely,

Sumi Park

Sumi Park

Encls.

Sample Cover Letter | 2

Susan Turner
125 Main St.
Vein, CO 23827
Tel. (478) 642 7565
susant@bdg.com

Nov. 5, 2014

Mr. Kevin Lui
Manager, Human Resources Dept.
Solar Law Firm
198 Eisenhower Rd.
Buffalo, NY 24387

Dear Mr. Kevin Lui:

I am writing to apply for the position of Executive Secretary which was advertised in the latest edition of *Today's Issue*. I am currently employed by a manufacturing company as a secretary but I'd like to pursue my career at your prestigious company.

As you will notice on the enclosed resume, I majored Business Administration acquiring all the basics of business. I work well under pressure and enjoy working in a team. In addition, I speak English fluently.

I would be available for interview at any time. Meanwhile, please do not hesitate to contact me if you need any further information. I look forward to hearing from you soon.

Sincerely,

Hyemi Kim

Hyemi Kim

Encl.

Job Interview Questions &Answers

인터뷰는 특히 철저한 사전 준비가 매우 중요한 취업의 단계라 할 수 있다. 질문에 적절히 대답할 수 있도록 예상 문제들을 뽑아 철저히 준비하고, 자신감 있는 태도를 가져야 한다.

1. 자신의 이력서와 지원서의 내용들을 잘 숙지하고 있어야 한다. 자신이 기재한 내용들에 관해 보다 구체적인 질문을 받을 수 있다.
2. 지원 회사에 대해 철저히 리서치 해야 한다. 최근 기사나 관련 보고서를 찾아 본다.
3. 자신이 면접관의 입장이 되어서 인터뷰 질문들을 예상해 본다.

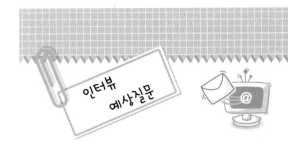

인터뷰
예상질문

 1. 자기소개 (Self-Introduction)

- ⓥ Introduce yourself briefly.
- ⓥ How would you describe yourself?
- ⓥ How would your friends describe you?
- ⓥ What are your short-term (or long-term) goals?

 2. 강점과 약점 (Strengths and Weaknesses)

- ⓥ What are your major strengths and weaknesses?
- ⓥ What are your own special abilities?

 3. 학력 (Academic Career)

- ⓥ What is your major?
- ⓥ Would you summarize your work history and education for me briefly?
- ⓥ Why did you choose ____전공____ as your major?
- ⓥ Your college transcript shows that your grades in the first year of college were not so good. Was there any particular reason?
- ⓥ Why is your GPA not higher?

203

 4. 학생활동, 사회활동 (Student Activity & Social Activity)

- Could you tell me something about your extracurricular activities in your school days?
- In what school activities have you participated? Why?

 5. 지원자격 (Job Qualification)

- Why should we employ you?
- How does your previous experience relate to this position?
- How has your experience prepared you for this job?
- What can you do for us that someone else can't do?
- What do you think is the essential trait that is needed for a (직업명: secretary)?
- What are your strengths for this job?

 6. 직업관 / 직업에 대한 태도 (Vocation View / Attitude Towards the Job)

- Why do you think we need a job?
- How would you describe the ideal job for you?
- What are you looking for in a job?
- How would you describe an ideal (직업명 : civil servant, secretary…)?
- What do you see yourself doing five years from now?
- What are your long-term career plans?
- Would you check voicemail and email when you are on vacation?

7. 직장경험 (Job Experiences)

- Have you ever worked before?
- Where have you worked?
- When did you work there?
- What were your responsibilities?
- How long have you been working there?
- Do you have work experience as a (secretary)?
- What have you learned from your past job?
- Why do you want to leave your current job?

8. 스트레스 관리 기술 (Stress Management Skills)

- How do you work under pressure?
- How do you deal with stressful situations?

9. 조직 적응력 (Organization Conformity)

- Do you prefer working with others or by yourself?
- How do you get on with others at work?
- What would you do when you have a problem with a co-worker or your boss?
- How would you describe your work style?

10. 지도력 (Leadership)

- Are you a leader or a follower?
- What type of leader do you admire and why?

11. 여가와 취미 (Leisure and Hobby)

- What do you do in your spare time?
- What's your hobby?
- How did you spend your vacations while in school?

 12. 인생관 (View of Life)

- What is the most important thing in your life?

 13. 지원동기 (Application Motivation)

- Why do you want to work here?
- What do you want from us?
- Why did you decide to seek a position with this company?

 14. 사전 지식 (Prior Knowledge)

- What do you know about our company?
- What is the worst thing you have heard about our company?
- What do you know about our products?

15. 책, 영화, 뉴스 (Books, Movies, News)

Describe a recent book or movie that you really identified with.

What was the last book you read or the last movie you saw and how did it affect you?

What do you think of the news surrounding (Kim OOO)?

Professional   전문의, 전문가

I'll try my best to support my boss and co-workers with a professional attitude. I think that a professional should quickly grasp what has to be done.

Hardworking   근면한, 부지런히 일하는

I am hardworking under any circumstances. Whatever I do, I go to great length to achieve my goals, and then I reward myself accordingly.

Outstanding   뛰어난

I have an outstanding ability to learn something speedily.

Multiple   다양한, 다방면의

I think multitasking is inevitable and natural. To manage multiple tasks, I will make an effective plan before getting started.

Qualified   자질이 있는, 적임의

I am fully qualified for the secretarial position.

Intensive   집약적인, 집중된

I completed office administration program and secretary training course. They were all intensive and interactive courses in which only ten students did some case studies.

Vital   매우 중요한

Punctuality is vital in workplaces because mutual trust basically starts from it.

Effective   효과적인

When I am at work, I don't waste time on website surfing which is not related to my work. To be effective in my work, I try to get rid of distractions around me.

Analytical   분석적인. 분석의

I am inclined to be analytical. It enables me to be prudent in every respect.

Accurate   정확한

To be accurate in my work, I make daily plans and weekly plans, and try to stick to them.

Invaluable   매우 귀중한

I worked as a part-timer during vacations, and actively participated in various volunteer programs. I gained invaluable hands-on experience while volunteering at a local community center.

Demanding   지나치게 요구하는

I am quite demanding with my work. So I always do my best to get satisfactory results.

Challenging   도전적인. 도전 의식을 북돋우는

I think I am really challenging. I enjoy doing something new and difficult, instead of running true to form.

Considerate   동정심 많은. 사려 깊은

I am always considerate of other's feeling.

Thoughtful   사려 깊은

I am quiet and thoughtful.

Open-minded   (새로운 생각 등을) 받아들이기 쉬운, 편견 없는

I think I am open-minded enough to learn something new.

I tend to listen to others with an open mind.

Decisive   과단성 있는, 단호한 (in a decisive manner 과감하게)

People say that I handle matters in a rapid and decisive manner.

Motivated   동기가 부여된 (highly motivated 의욕이 강한)

I am a highly-motivated and well-trained candidate for a secretarial position.

Cheerful   쾌활한

I consider myself a cheerful person. I mix well in any company.

Honest   솔직한

I am honest and fair. So if I make a mistake, I fully apologize for it with no excuses, and then make up for the mistake.

Active   활동적인, 활발한

I am a very energetic person who tries to do something all the time. My friends often tell me that I am very active.

Organized   사람이 체계적인

I think I am well organized. When I am given a task, I always plan ahead. So my planner is always filled with detailed schedules and plans. I update the planner as often as necessary to make fewer mistakes.

Creative   창의적인

Whenever there's a problem to be solved, I try to come up with a solution from a different point of view. So people frequently say that I am very creative.

Competitive   경쟁의, 경쟁심이 강한

My parents say I am competitive by nature. I think I am especially competitive with myself. So I tend to push myself to get the best results.

Self-initiated   자신이 주도적으로 시작하는

I was a self-initiated student in my school years. For example, I completed Professional Secretary Training Program, Business English Diploma Program and Office Administration Diploma Program. .

Self-starter   자발적으로 행동하는 사람

I am a self-starter. That explains why I look for new things, and try to act on my own initiative.

Interpersonal   대인 관계의

I have pretty good interpersonal skills. So I've had good relationships with my friends and family members. My interpersonal skills will be a great asset in my workplace in the future.

Sociable   사교적인, 붙임성 있는

I am a sociable person. So I can make friends easily.

Intellectual   지적인

People around me say that I am intellectual. I think it is because I am interested in learning new things.

Witty   재치있는

I am good at lightening up the atmosphere. My friends say that I have a witty sense of humor.

Independent 독립적인

I am very independent. I have earned most of my college tuition. It is why I have a lot of part time job experience with little voluntary work experience.

Dependable 믿을 수 있는

People say that I am so dependable. When I worked part-time at a convenience store, I was in charge of inventory management. When the store owner went on vacation for three days, he left everything up to me saying that I am so dependable.

Integrated (인격이) 원만한, 융화된

I think I am a person with a balanced and integrated personality.

Listen to others 남의 말에 귀 기울이다

I tend to listen to others rather than talk about my opinion.

Warm-hearted 마음이 따뜻한, 인간미 있는

I am a warm-hearted person and I like to do something for others.

Affable 상냥한, 사근사근한

I am affable. So my friends say I am easy to get along with.

Dutiful 의무를 다하는, 착실한

I am dutiful. Basically, I do everything that I have to do. And then I seek for what I can do further.

Discreet 신중한, 조심스러운

I am discreet in talking. So some of my friends disclose their secrets to me.

Meticulous 꼼꼼한, 세심한

When I begin something new, I create a plan with meticulous attention to detail.

Understanding   이해심있는

I am a very understanding person. I try to be in other's shoe.

Trustworthy   믿을 수 있는

In my school years, I was considered trustworthy. So some important work was given to me.

Confident   자신감 있는

I am confident about my ability to do the job.

Can-do attitude   의욕적인 태도

My can-do attitude will help me to win the hearts of other people in the workplace.

Articulate   생각을 분명히 표현하다 / 분명히 표현하는

I am good at articulating my thoughts.

Traits   특성

These traits of mine will help me to become a competent secretary.

Adaptability and compatibility   적응력과 친화성

I have a strong adaptability and compatibility. I can easily acknowledge and accept differences among people. These character traits enable me to get along with any kind of people.

 교육, 졸업, 전공 관련 표현 ·····························

▼ I graduated from (학교명) in (연도) with a major in (전공) and a minor in (부전공).

저는 (   )년도에 (   )학교를 졸업하였으며, (   )를 전공으로 하고, (   )을 부전공으로 하였습니다.

▼ I will be graduated from (학교명) next semester.

저는 다음 학기에 (   )를 졸업하게 됩니다.

▼ I graduated with excellent grades.

저는 좋은 성적으로 졸업하였습니다.

▼ I received my (학위명) from (학교명) with a (학점) GPA.

저는 (학교명)로부터 (학점)성적으로 (학위명)을 받았습니다.

▼ I graduated with 3.9 GPA in 2014. It was based on a 4.0 scale.

저는 2014년도 GPA(Grade Point Average) 3.9로 졸업했습니다.
4.0만점 기준입니다.

▼ I graduated with top honors.

저는 우등으로 졸업하였습니다.

▼ I have recently completed (professional secretary training) course provided by (학교 또는기관명).

저는 최근에는 (학교 또는 기관명)에서 주관하는 (전문비서 양성) 과정을 마쳤습니다.

▼ I am currently taking (강좌명).

저는 요즘 (   )수업을 듣고 있습니다.

기술이나 자질에 대한 표현

I speak fluent English and a little of Chinese.
저는 영어를 유창하게 하고 중국어를 조금합니다.

I am proficient in MS Word and PowerPoint.
저는 MS word 와 PowerPoint를 잘 합니다.

I am creative, detail-oriented, imaginative and dedicated to perfection.
저는 창의적이고, 꼼꼼하고, 상상력이 풍부하며, 완벽을 기합니다.

I can type quickly and accurately.
저는 타이핑을 빠르고 정확하게 할 수 있습니다.

I have an ability to multitask.
저는 동시에 여러 가지 일을 처리하는 능력이 있습니다.

I have excellent time-management and prioritization skills.
저는 시간관리 능력과 일의 우선 순위를 결정하는 능력이 있습니다.

I seldom leave a task unfinished once I have started it.
저는 일단 시작하면 일을 끝내지 않는 경우는 거의 없습니다.

I can perfectly use a variety of computer software programs.
다양한 컴퓨터 소프트웨어 프로그램을 사용할 수 있습니다.

 경력, 경험 관련 표현

▼ I was involved in various extracurricular activities. Firstly, I was the vice president of the student council at my college. While working for the student council, I experienced various administrative works. I was also able to learn collaboration with other students. Secondly, I worked part time at a convenience store as a cashier. In summer, I worked as a receptionist at an English Language Institute. I could learn how to be polite and patient while dealing with customers' complaints at a convenience store. While working for the English Language Institute, I had plenty of opportunities to communicate with native English speaking teachers and I could improve my English. Thirdly, I regularly volunteered to work at an elderly care facility. My experience there was very rewarding. It gave me joy and made me feel appreciated for everything around me.

저는 다양한 과외 활동을 하였습니다. 첫 번째로 학생회 부회장을 하였습니다. 학생회 일을 하면서, 다양한 행정 일을 경험하였습니다. 다른 학생들과의 협력도 배울 수 있었습니다. 두 번째로 편의점에서 계산대 직원으로 아르바이트를 하였습니다. 여름에는 영어학원에서 접수담당자로 일하였습니다. 편의점에서 고객들의 불평을 처리하면서 어떻게 하면 예의바른지와 인내하는 법을 배웠습니다. 영어학원에서 일하면서는 원어민 영어 말하기 선생님들과 의사소통 할 기회를 쉽게 얻을 수 있어서 영어 실력을 향상시킬 수 있었습니다. 세 번째로 저는 노인 요양 시설에서 규칙적으로 자원봉사 하였습니다. 그 곳에서의 경험은 아주 보람 있었습니다. 그것은 저에게 즐거움을 주었고 제 주변 모든 것에 감사함을 느낄 수 있게 해 주었습니다.

▼ I started doing voluntary work in 2009 at an orphanage and I am still doing it regularly. Now I also work for tutoring and mentoring program for elementary school students. I've realized that voluntary work doesn't just benefit the people whom I am working for, but it benefits me in the end. In addition, I can get opportunites to meet new people while doing voluntary work.

저는 2009년 한 고아원에서 자원봉사활동을 처음 시작하였는데, 지금까지도 규칙적으로 하고 있습니다. 지금은 또한 초등학생을 위한 Tutoring & Mentoring Program을 위해 일하고 있습니다. 자원봉사는 제가 일을 해 드리는 분에게만 득이 되는 것이 아니고, 결국에는 저에게 득이 되는 일임을 깨달았습니다. 게다가 자원봉사를 하면서 새로운 사람을 만날 기회도 얻을 수 있습니다.

Ⓥ I have prepared myself to become a competent secretary. Firstly, I thought English language podcasts would be an excellent way to improve my English. So every day I listened to podcasts on my smartphone during commuting hours. I also have been taking several Business English courses at my college for two years. Secondly, I worked part time at my college library ten hours a week. My main role was keeping the library organized and tidy. I sometimes helped students find what they were searching for and assisted librarians' administrative duties. So I expect I will quickly learn basic office skills. Thirdly, I completed Professional Secretary Training Course at my college.

저는 능력 있는 비서가 되기 위해 저 자신을 준비해 왔습니다. 우선 저는 영어실력을 향상시키 위해서 영어 팟캐스트가 좋은 방법이라고 생각했습니다. 그래서 매일 등하교 길에 스마트폰으로 팟캐스트를 들었습니다. 또한 학교에서 2년 동안 몇 가지 비즈니스 영어 과정들을 수강해오고 있습니다. 두 번째로 일주일에 10시간 학교 도서관에서 파트 타임으로 일을 했습니다. 저의 주된 역할은 도서관을 정리하고 깨끗하게 유지하는 것이었습니다. 때때로 학생들이 찾는 것을 찾도록 도와주기도 했고, 사서들의 행정적인 일들도 도왔습니다. 그래서 기본적인 사무실 업무는 빨리 배울 것 같습니다. 세 번째로 저는 학교에서 전문 비서 과정을 수료하였습니다.

Ⓥ I have considerable experience in customer service. It was not at all easy to deal with demanding customers. While working there, I learned to accept other people's differences and became resistant to stress.

저는 고객 서비스 관련 상당한 경험을 갖고 있습니다. 까다로운 고객을 다루는 일은 결코 쉽지 않았습니다. 거기서 일하면서 남들의 다른 점을 받아들이는 것을 배웠고, 스트레스를 잘 견디게 되었습니다.

☑ While at A&G, I could sharpen my skills as a secretary.

A&G에서 일하면서, 비서로서 자질을 갈고 닦을 수 있었습니다.

☑ In that position, I was able to develop interpersonal relationship skills.

그 자리에 있으면서 대인관계 기술을 개발할 수 있었습니다.

☑ Through the overseas internship program, I've gained practical work experience and improved my English.

해외 인턴쉽 프로그램을 통해 실무경험을 얻고, 영어를 향상 시켰습니다.

☑ I volunteered to work at the 19th Busan International Film Festival from October 2 to 11 in 2014.

저는 2014년 10월 2일부터 11일까지 19회 부산국제 영화제에서 자원봉사를 하였습니다.

☑ I performed typing and other administrative duties.

타이핑 및 기타 행정 업무를 했었습니다.

☑ I was responsible for data entry, website management and all general office duties.

저는 자료입력, 웹사이트 관리 그리고 일반적 사무 업무를 담당했었습니다.

(filing, faxing, mailing letters, post sorting, creating reports or letters 등도 업무내용으로 쓸 수 있다.)

장기적 목표

V Within ten years, I would like to become the very best secretary in this company.

10년 내에, 저는 이 회사 최고의 비서가 되고 싶습니다.

V Ten years from now I see myself still working hard as a secretary.

저는 지금부터 10년 뒤에도 여전히 비서로써 열심히 일하고 있을 제가 보입니다..

V I want to stay in this company and make a significant advance in the administration.

저는 이 회사에 있으면서 행정 분야에서 크게 성장하고 싶습니다.

V My goal is to be a top-level professional in my field and I want to be satisfied with my life. Balancing between my own personal life and professional life will be the key.

저의 목표는 저의 분야에서 최고 전문가가 되는 것이며 저의 삶에서도 만족하고 싶습니다. 개인으로 서 저의 삶과 직업인으로서 저의 삶에 균형을 맞추는 것이 관건일 것입니다.

I think secretarial job is a good fit for me. I am good at organizing, planning, paying attention to details, multi-tasking and prioritizing. Actually I always make a list of my daily duties, and prioritize them. I think these qualifications perfectly suit secretarial position.

저는 비서직에 적임자라고 생각합니다. 저는 정리, 계획을 잘하고, 세부사항에 주의를 기울이고, 여러 가지 일을 동시에 잘 하며, 일의 우선 순위를 매기는 것도 잘 합니다. 사실 저는 그 날에 할 일들의 목록을 항상 만들고, 그 일들의 우선 순위를 매깁니다. 이러한 자질들은 비서직에 완벽히 맞다고 생각합니다.

I would like to say I have great interpersonal skills. I am both sociable and reliable. Secretaries can easily get access to confidential documents. So secretaries should be reliable, and I believe that I am the very reliable person.

저는 제가 대인관계 능력이 아주 좋다고 생각합니다. 저는 사교적이면서도 믿을만한 사람입니다. 비서들은 기밀 보고서를 쉽게 접할 수 있습니다. 그래서 비서들은 믿을만 해야 할 것이고, 제가 바로 그 믿을만한 사람이라고 믿습니다.

I am sure I can always be reached in an emergency, even if other people cover for me during vacation.

휴가 중에는 다른 사람들이 저를 대신해서 일하겠지만, 비상시에는 항상 연락될 수 있다고 확신합니다.

The ideal job would be the one in which I can fully utilize my talents.

이상적인 직업은 저의 재능을 마음껏 발휘할 수 있는 곳일 것입니다.

I want to work for a company which encourages my professional growth.

제가 직업적으로 성장할 수 있게 해 주는 회사에서 일하고 싶습니다.

지도력, 화합적 성격

Ⓥ I like working alone when I need to have concentration. However, I also enjoy working with people with different ideas and perspectives. I like being a part of a team under a common goal. Most of all, I like getting close to teammates while working together.

집중력이 필요할 때는 혼자 일하는 것을 좋아합니다. 그러나 다른 생각과 관점을 가진 사람과 같이 일하는 것도 좋아합니다. 공동의 목표 하에 팀의 일원이 되는 것이 좋습니다. 무엇보다도 같이 일하면서 팀 동료들과 가까워지는 것이 좋습니다.

Ⓥ Throughout my school years, I have been frequently required to complete group assignments with my classmates. While completing those team projects, I could learn how to communicate effectively with others and mediate conflicts among team members. I enjoyed those group assignments. I think those experiences will provide a valuable aid when I work with other people.

학교 다니면서 반 친구들과 그룹과제를 해야 하는 경우가 자주 있었습니다. 그 팀 프로젝트들을 완성해 가면서 다른 사람과 효율적으로 의사 소통하는 법과 팀 원들간의 갈등을 조정하는 법을 배울 수 있었습니다. 저는 그 그룹과제들을 즐겁게 하였습니다. 그러한 경험들은 제가 다른 사람들과 일할 때, 매우 유익한 도움을 줄 것이라 생각합니다.

Ⓥ Sometimes I lead a team but other times I follow a leader. It depends on the situation.

때로는 제가 팀을 이끌기도 하고, 때로는 리더를 따르기도 합니다. 상황에 따라 다릅니다.

Ⓥ I am more of a leader than a follower when working with colleagues in a team.

저는 팀에서 동료들과 일할 때, 따라가는 사람이라기 보다는 이끌어가는 사람입니다.

Ⓥ When working with other people, I frequently take on additional responsibilities.

다른 사람들과 일할 때, 저는 종종 추가적인 책임을 떠 맡습니다.

 I was a member of movie discussion club during my college years. The club activity enabled me to make new friends who share the same interests. While exchanging ideas with the club members, I could widen my understanding of other people and their ideas.

저는 대학 때 영화토론 동아리의 멤버였습니다. 동아리 활동은 같은 관심사를 가진 새로운 친구들을 만나게 해 주었습니다. 동아리 멤버들과 생각을 나누면서 저는 다른 사람과 그들의 생각에 대한 이해의 폭을 넓힐 수 있었습니다.

 I really wanted to improve my English speaking skills. So I was in English speaking club.

저는 영어로 말하는 기술을 향상시키고 싶었습니다. 그래서 영어 말하기 동아리에 가입했었습니다.

여가활동

☑ When I am given an unexpected free time, I sometimes travel alone. It is because I can hardly accmmodate myself to someone else's schedule. Travelling alone was not so bad. I went backpacking in Europe by myself last year.

예상치못한 여가시간이 주어지면, 저는 때때로 혼자 여행을 합니다. 다른 사람의 일정에 제 자신을 맞추기가 무척 어렵기 때문입니다. 혼자 여행하는 것이 그리 나쁘지 않았습니다. 작년에는 혼자서 유럽 배낭 여행을 갔었습니다.

☑ Actually, I have very little spare time. But if I have a lot of free time, I want to go out to have fun. And if I am given just one or two hours of free time, I'll allow myself to do nothing. I think recharging my energy would also help me go further.

사실상 저는 여가 시간이 거의 없습니다. 그러나 만약 많은 자유시간이 있다면 나가서 즐기고 싶습니다. 그리고 한 두 시간의 자유시간이 주어지면, 저 자신에게 아무것도 안 하도록 하고 허용해주고 싶습니다. 에너지를 재충전 하는 것 또한 제가 더 나아가는 데 있어서 도움이 될 것이라 생각 합니다.

☑ I love reading non-fiction books and the last book that I read was the autobiography of the social worker ~.

저는 논픽션 책을 읽기를 좋아하며, 마지막으로 읽은 책은 유명 사회사업가~의 자서전 입니다.

☑ I like outdoor activities, especially mountain hiking. So I joined various online communities and meet the members on weekends.

저는 바깥 활동 특히 등산을 좋아합니다. 그래서 다양한 온라인 동호회에 가입하여 주말에는 동호회 회원들을 만납니다.

☑ I usually hang out with my friends.

주로 친구들과 어울립니다.

☑ I like going to the movies with my friends.

친구들과 영화 보러 가는 것을 좋아합니다

☑ I think I have qualifications required for a secretarial position. For one thing, when I do something with other people, I listen to others first, and then express my opinion.

저는 비서직에 필요한 자질을 갖고 있다고 생각합니다. 우선 한 가지는, 제가 다른 사람과 뭔가를 할 때, 먼저 남의 말을 듣고 나서 제 의견을 표현한다는 것입니다.

☑ My strength is that I make friends easily. So I can adapt myself to new circumstances quickly.

제 장점은 쉽게 사람들을 사귀는 것입니다. 그래서 저는 새로운 환경에 빨리 적응할 수 있습니다.

☑ I am always thorough and detail-oriented at my work. Sometimes my perfectionism makes me tired. But in most cases, it enables me to work meticulously.

저는 언제나 일을 철저하고 꼼꼼하게 합니다. 가끔은 완벽주의가 저를 피곤하게도 합니다. 그러나 대부분의 경우에 꼼꼼하게 일 할 수 있도록 해 줍니다.

☑ My weakness is that I don't like to leave something half-done. I can't concentrate on anything else until one thing is finished. But instead, I make fewer mistakes when a high level of accuracy is required.

저는 어떤 일을 반쯤 하다가 남겨두는 것을 싫어합니다. 저는 하나의 일이 끝나기 전에는 다른 일에 집중할 수가 없습니다. 그러나 대신에 높은 수준의 정확성이 요구될 때 실수를 덜 합니다.

☑ I am so careful and prudent that I usually take much time before making any decision. But once I make the decision, I just push ahead with it and never look back.

저는 너무 조심스럽고 신중한 면이 있어서 결정을 하는 데 너무 많은 시간을 씁니다. 그러나 일단 결정하면 그냥 추진하며 되돌아 보지 않습니다..

Business English for Secretaries

I am hardworking and never lose self-confidence at any moment.
저는 부지런히 일하고 어떤 순간에도 자신감을 잃지 않습니다

Most of all, I quickly and easily accept changes.
무엇보다도 변화를 빠르고 쉽게 받아들입니다.

인생관

My family is the most important thing in my life. My health is also important, so I exercise regularly.
저의 삶에서 가족이 제일 중요합니다. 저의 건강도 중요해서 규칙적으로 운동합니다.

Most of all, I think life should be fun. So I try to have a lot of fun every day and I enjoy learning new things.
무엇보다도 삶은 즐거운 것이라야 한다고 생각합니다. 그래서 매일 많은 즐거움을 경험하려고 하며, 새로운 것들을 배우기를 즐깁니다.

My motto is "There are no shortcuts to success." I think that hard work and perseverance are the basis to achieve something worthwhile in my life.
저의 좌우명은 "성공에는 지름길이 없다"는 것입니다. 저의 삶에서 뭔가 가치있는 것을 이루기 위해서는 열심히 일하고 인내하는 것이 기본이라고 생각합니다.

BUSINESS
ENGLiISH for
SECRETARIES

References

References

 Department Name (부서명)

- 📢 General Affairs Dept.   총무부
- 📢 Marketing Dept.   마켓팅부
- 📢 Accounting Dept.   회계부
- 📢 Public Relations Dept. (PR)   홍보부
- 📢 Human Resources Dept. (HR)   인사부
- 📢 Personnel Dept.   인사부
- 📢 Sales Dept.   영업부
- 📢 Planning Dept.   기획부
- 📢 Financial Dept.   재무부
- 📢 Research and Development Dept. (R& D Dept.)   연구개발부
- 📢 Legal Affairs Dept.   법무부
- 📢 Purchasing Dept.   구매부
- 📢 Advertising Dept.   광고부
- 📢 Customer Service   고객관리
- 📢 Headquarters(HQ)   본사
- 📢 Branch Office   지사, 지점

회사 관련 용어

▶▶ Inc. (=incorporated)   주식회사

▶▶ Ltd. (=limited)   유한회사

▶▶ multinational company   다국적기업

▶▶ corporate   기업의

▶▶ corporation (= enterprise, firm)   기업

▶▶ conglomerate   대기업

▶▶ joint venture company   합작회사

▶▶ small and medium-sized enterprise (SME)   중소기업

▶▶ headquarters   본사

▶▶ branch   지사

▶▶ subsidiary (company)   자회사

▶▶ affiliate (company)   계열사

▶▶ holdings   지주회사

▶▶ parent company   모회사

Position Name (직위명)

▶◀ Organization Chart   조직표

▶◀ Chairman   회장

▶◀ Vice Chairman   부회장

▶◀ Board of Directors   이사회

▶◀ CEO (Chief Executive Officer)   최고경영자

▶◀ CFO (Chief Financial Officer)   최고재무경영자

▶◀ President   사장

▶◀ Vice President (VP)   부사장

▶◀ Executive   이사, 중역

▶◀ Managing Director (MD)   상무이사

▶◀ General Manager   부장

▶◀ Deputy General Manager   차장

▶◀ Assistant Manager   대리

▶◀ Staff/Associate/Clerk   사원

▶◀ Secretary   비서

▶◀ Receptionist   안내

은행 업무 관련 용어

- deposit   입금하다, 예금

- withdraw   출금하다

- transfer   송금하다

- teller   은행 수납원

- ATM (Automated Teller Machine)   자동 입출금기

- savings account   입금 계좌

- checking account   당좌 계좌

- open an account   계좌를 만들다

- monthly statement   월별 명세서

- balance   잔고

- checkbook   수표책

- passbook   통장

- PIN (Personal Identification Number)   개인 비밀번호

- safety box   금고

- security guard   청원 경찰

 무역, 회계 관련 용어

- 개인표   personal check
- 고정자산   non-current assets
- 관세   tariff
- 국민순생산   Net National Product (NNP)
- 금수조치   embargo
- 대출   loan
- 도매가   wholesale price
- 매도인   seller
- 매수인   buyer
- 변상   reimbursement
- 보험료   premium
- 보험증서   insurance policy
- 선적/발송   shipment
- 세금영수증/계산서   tax invoice
- 순이익   net profit
- 액면가액   face value
- 이자   interest
- 위임장   power of attorney
- 자본준비금   capital reserves
- 재고자산   inventories
- 재무제표   financial statements
- 전환사채   convertible bonds
- 저축예금   savings deposit
- 지적소유권   intellectual property rights
- 총이익   gross profit

- 투자자산   investments
- 회계연도   fiscal year
- 공모발행   public offering
- 국공채   public bond
- 국민총생산   Gross National Product (GNP)
- 개인소득세   individual income tax
- 당좌자산   quick assets
- 독점계약   exclusive contract
- 무역/통상   trade
- 배당/이윤   return
- 보험 약관   policy statements
- 부가가치세   value added tax (VAT)
- 부채   liabilities
- 선급금   advance payments
- 선물거래   futures trading
- 손실   loss
- 손익계산서   statement of profit and loss
- 손익분기점   break-even point
- 수혜자   beneficiary
- 신용장   letter of credit (L/C)
- 운임   freight
- 자본   capital
- 자산   assets
- 장기부채   long-term liabilities
- 증권거래소   stock exchange
- 통관   customs clearance
- 총액지급   lump-sum payment
- 현물상환방식   cash on delivery (COD)

Business English for Secretaries

 ADD   addess

 ADMIN   administration

 APP   application

 A.S.A.P.   As soon as possible

 a.k.a.   also known as

 ATM   Automated Teller Machine

 BTW   By the way

 BOE   Board of Executives

 BYOD   Bring Your Own Device

 CEO   Chief Executive Officer

 CFO   Chief Financial Officer

 COD   Cash on Delivery

 CPA   Certified Public Accountant

 CPU   Central Processing Unit

 CV   Curriculum Vitae

 DIY   Do It Yourself

 DOB   Date of Birth

 DST   Daylight Saving Time

 FAQ   Frequently Asked Question

- **FYI** For Your Information

- **GDP** Gross Domestic Product

- **GNP** Gross National Product

- **GmbH** "Company with limited liability"

- **GPA** Grade Point Average

- **ISP** Internet Service Provider

- **IT** Information Technology

- **IPO** Initial Public Offering

- **LCD** Liquid Crystal Display

- **MA** Master of Arts

- **M&A** Merger and Acquisition

- **MD** Medical Doctor

- **MOU** Memorandum of Understanding

- **NGO** Non-Government Organization

- **N/A** Not Available, Not Applicable

- **OS** Operating System

- **P&L** Profit and Loss

- **ROI** Return on Investment

- **R.S.V.P.** "Please reply"

- **SNS** Social Network Service

- **TBA** To Be Announced

- **VM** Voice Mail

- **www** World Wide Web

Punctuations

.	?	!	" "
Period	Question mark	Exclamation mark	Quotation marks
-	—	/	( )
Hyphen	Dash	Slash	Parentheses
,	'	:	;
Comma	Apostrophe	Colon	Semicolon

A period marks the end of the sentence.

Question mark shows there is some doubt.

Exclamation mark expresses emphasis or surprise.

Quotation marks are used to show what someone actually said.

Hyphen is used for word-division or word-joining.

Dash is used to separate ideas or words — usually added as an afterthought.

Slash is used to show alternatives and separate them.

Parentheses are used when the words are not of primary importance.

Comma is like a pause.

Apostrophe is used in possessives.

Colon is to emphasize what is coming next or to list things.

Semicolon can be used to separate two sentences when they are closely connected.

Operations

Addition (덧셈)	12 + 4 = 16	Twelve plus four is [equals] sixteen. Twelve and four is [makes] sixteen.
Subtraction (뺄셈)	12 - 4 = 8	Twelve minus four is [equals] eight.
Multiplication (곱셈)	12 × 4 = 48	Twelve times four is [equals] forty eight.
Division (나눗셈)	12 / 3 = 4	Twelve divided by three is [equals] four.

숫자 읽기

 ### 분수

분수를 읽을 때 분모는 서수로 분자는 기수로 읽고 분자가 2이상이면 분모의
서수에 –s를 붙인다.

- 1/2   a half
- 1/3   one third
- 2/3   two thirds

소수

소수를 읽을 때 소수점은 point로 읽는다.

- 0.5   point five
- 2.78   two point seven eight

큰 수 읽기

숫자는 comma (,) 단위로 끊어 읽는다.

24, 354, 554, 903, 924

Trillion, billion, million, thousand

Twenty four trillion, three hundred fifty four billion, five hundred fifty four
million, nine hundred three thousand, (and) nine hundred twenty four.

제곱수 읽기

- $3^2 = 9$ Three squared is nine.
- $3^3 = 27$ Three cubed is twenty seven.
- $3^4 = 81$ Three to the fourth (power) is eighty one.

2D & 3D Shapes

Business English for Secretaries

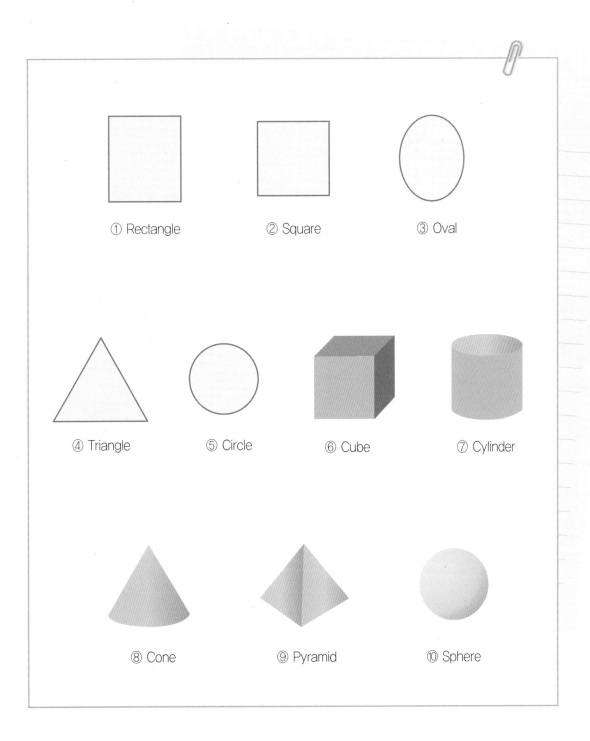

① Rectangle   ② Square   ③ Oval

④ Triangle   ⑤ Circle   ⑥ Cube   ⑦ Cylinder

⑧ Cone   ⑨ Pyramid   ⑩ Sphere

저자 소개

김 영 지

- 이화여자대학교 영어영문학과 졸업
- 이화여자대학교 교육대학원 영어교육전공 교육학 석사
- 한양대학교 영어교육과 박사과정 수료
- 숭실대, 수원과학대학, 한양여자대학 강의

권 은 희

- 이화여자대학교 영어영문학과 졸업
- 이화여자대학교 영어영문학과 문학석사
- 美 Eastern Michigan University TESOL 석사
- 고려대학교 영어교육과 박사과정 수료
- 숭실대, 수원과학대학 강의

비서를 위한 **비즈니스 영어**

초판1쇄 발행 2015년 5월 20일
초판3쇄 발행 2020년 2월 20일

지은이 김영지 · 권은희
펴낸이 임 순 재

펴낸곳 **주식회사 한올출판사**
등 록 제11-403호
주 소 서울시 마포구 모래내로 83 (성산동, 한올빌딩 3층)
전 화 (02)376-4298(대표)
팩 스 (02)302-8073
홈페이지 www.hanol.co.kr
e-메일 hanol@hanol.co.kr

값 15,000원   ISBN 979-11-5685-080-9